P9-CCP-674

A HISTORICAL READER

Slavery
IN AMERICA

nextext

Printed in the United States of America

ISBN 0-618-04822-7

1 2 3 4 5 6 7 — QKT — 06 05 04 03 02 01 00

Table of Contents

*Throughout the reader, vocabulary words appear in boldface
type and are footnoted. Specialized or technical words and phrases
appear in lightface type and are footnoted.*

chapter 1

Coming from Africa

from

Roots

BY ALEX HALEY

*In the more than 135 years since the end of the Civil War,
historians and scholars have studied the institution of slavery.
They have examined the writing and narratives of former slaves,
the business and personal records of slave owners, slave laws
and court proceedings, and newspapers from the slavery era.
The following account describes a prominent African-American
writer's search for his ancestors and his African roots.*

*Alexander Palmer Haley (1921–1992) was himself a part of
modern African-American history. He was co-author, with
Malcolm X, of* The Autobiography of Malcolm X *(1965), a book
that won Haley international recognition. But the work that made
Haley a household name did not appear until 1976. Haley's*
Roots: The Saga of an American Family *was an immediate
bestseller, winning many literary awards—including a Pulitzer
Prize. The story subsequently was dramatized in a widely watched
television film, entered the American imagination, and helped
illuminate one of the darkest and most painful periods in the
history of the United States.*

The Childhood Memory

I suppose it was somehow to try to fill the void of Grandpa's absence that now during each springtime, Grandma began to invite various ones among the Murray family female relatives to spend some, if not all, of the summers with us. Averaging in her age range, the late forties and early fifties, they came from exotic-sounding places to me, such as Dyersburg, Tennessee; Inkster, Michigan; St. Louis and Kansas City—and they had names like Aunt Plus, Aunt Liz, Aunt Till, Aunt Viney, and Cousin Georgia. With the supper dishes washed, they all would go out on the front porch and sit in cane-bottomed rocking chairs, and I would be among them and sort of scrunch myself down behind the white-painted rocker holding Grandma. The time would be just about as the dusk was deepening into the night, with the lightning bugs flickering on and off around the honeysuckle vines, and every evening I can remember, unless there was some local priority gossip, always they would talk about the same things— snatches and patches of what later I'd learn was the long, **cumulative**[1] family narrative that had been passed down across the generations.

It was the talk, I knew, that always had generated my only memories of any open friction between Mama and Grandma. Grandma would get on that subject sometime without her older women summer guests there, and Mama always before long would abruptly snap something like, "Oh, Maw, I *wish* you'd stop all that old-timey slavery stuff, it's entirely embarrassing!" Grandma would snap right back, "If *you* don't care who and where you come from, well, *I* does!" And they might go around avoiding speaking to each other for a whole day, maybe even longer.

---

[1] **cumulative**—added to over time.

But anyway, I know I gained my initial impression that whatever Grandma and the other graying ladies talked about was something that went a very long way back when one or another of them would be recalling something of girlhood and suddenly thrusting a finger down toward me say, "I wasn't any bigger'n this here young'un!" The very idea that anyone as old and wrinkled as they had once been my age strained my comprehension. But as I say, it was this that caused me to realize that the things they were discussing must have happened a very long time ago.

Being just a little boy, I couldn't really follow most of what they said. I didn't know what an "ol' massa"[2] or an "ol' missis" was; I didn't know what a "plantation" was, though it seemed something resembling a farm. But slowly, from hearing the stories each passing summer, I began to recognize frequently repeated names among the people they talked about and to remember things they told about those people. The farthest-back person they ever talked about was a man they called "the African," whom they always said had been brought to this country on a ship to some place that they pro-nounced "'Naplis." They said he was bought off this ship by a "Massa John Waller," who had a plantation in a place called "Spotsylvania County, Virginia." They would tell how the African kept trying to escape, and how on the fourth effort he had the misfortune to be captured by two white professional slave catchers, who apparently decided to make an example of him. This African was given the choice either of being castrated[3] or having a foot cut off, and—"thanks to Jesus, or we wouldn't be here tellin' it"—the African chose his foot. I couldn't figure out why white folks would do anything as mean and low-down as that.

---

[2] "ol' massa"—old master, in southern U.S. dialect.

[3] **castrated**—having his testicles removed and thus being made unable to father children.

But this African's life, the old ladies said, had been saved by Massa John's brother, a Dr. William Waller, who was so mad about the entirely unnecessary maiming that he bought the African for his own plantation. Though now the African was crippled, he could do limited work, and the doctor assigned him in the vegetable garden. That was how it happened that this particular African was kept on one plantation for quite a long time—in a time when slaves, especially male slaves, were sold back and forth so much that slave children grew up often without even knowledge of who their parents were.

Grandma and the others said that Africans fresh off slave ships were given some name by their massas. In this particular African's case the name was "Toby." But they said anytime any of the other slaves called him that, he would strenuously rebuff them, declaring that his name was "Kin-tay."

Hobbling about, doing his gardening work, then later becoming his massa's buggy driver, "Toby"—or "Kin-tay"—met and eventually mated with a woman slave there whom Grandma and the other ladies called "Bell, the big-house cook." They had a little girl who was given the name "Kizzy." When she was around four to five years old, her African father began to take her by the hand and lead her around, whenever he got the chance, pointing out different things to her and repeating to her their names in his own native tongue. He would point at a guitar, for example, and say something that sounded like "*ko.*" Or he would point at the river that ran near the plantation—actually the Mattaponi River— and say what sounded like "Kamby Bolongo," along with many more things and sounds. As Kizzy grew older, and her African father learned English better, he began telling her stories about himself, his people, and his homeland—and how he was taken away from it. He said that he had been out in the forest not far from his village, chopping wood to make a drum, when he had been surprised by four men, overwhelmed, and kidnapped into slavery.

When Kizzy was sixteen years old, Grandma Palmer and the other Murray family ladies said, she was sold away to a new master named Tom Lea, who owned a small plantation in North Carolina. And it was on this plantation that Kizzy gave birth to a boy, whose father was Tom Lea, who gave the boy the name of George.

When George got around four or five years old, his mother began to tell him her African father's sounds and stories, until he came to know them well. Then when George got to be the age of twelve, I learned there on Grandma's front porch, he was apprenticed to an old "Uncle Mingo," who trained the master's fighting gamecocks,[4] and by the mid-teens, the youth had earned such a reputation as a gamecock trainer that he'd been given by others the nickname he'd take to his grave: "Chicken George."

Chicken George when around eighteen met and mated with a slave girl named Matilda, who in time bore him eight children. With each new child's birth, said Grandma and the others, Chicken George would gather his family within their slave cabin, telling them afresh about their African great-grandfather named "Kin-tay," who called a guitar a "*ko*," a river in Virginia "Kamby Bolongo," and other sounds for other things, and who had said he was chopping wood to make a drum when he was captured into slavery.

The eight children grew up, took mates, and had their own children. The fourth son, Tom, was a blacksmith when he was sold along with the rest of his family to a "Massa Murray," who owned a tobacco plantation in Alamance County, North Carolina. There, Tom met and mated with a half-Indian slave girl named Irene,

---

[4] gamecocks—roosters trained for cockfighting.

who came from the plantation of a "Massa Holt," who owned a cotton mill. Irene eventually also bore eight children, and with each new birth, Tom continued the tradition his father, Chicken George, had begun, gathering his family around the hearth and telling them about their African great-great-grandfather and all those descending from him.

Of that second set of eight children, the youngest was a little girl named Cynthia, who was two years old when her father, Tom, and grandfather, Chicken George, led a wagon train of recently freed slaves westward to Henning, Tennessee, where Cynthia met and at the age of twenty-two married Will Palmer.

When I had been thoroughly immersed in listening to accounts of all those people unseen who had lived away back yonder, invariably it would astonish me when the long narrative finally got down to Cynthia . . . and there I sat looking right at Grandma! As well as Aunt Viney, Aunt Matilda, and Aunt Liz, who had ridden right along with Grandma—her older sisters—in the wagon train.

*   *   *

Inspiration

. . . [Much later, while I was working as a writer] a magazine sent me on an assignment to London. Between appointments, utterly fascinated with a wealth of history everywhere, I missed scarcely a guided tour anywhere within London's area during the next several days. Poking about one day in the British Museum, I found myself looking at something I'd heard of vaguely: the Rosetta Stone. I don't know why, it just about entranced me. I got a book there in the museum library to learn more about it.

Discovered in the Nile delta, I learned, the stone's face had chiseled into it three separate texts: one in known Greek characters, the second in a then-unknown set of characters, the third in the ancient **hieroglyphics**,[5] which it had been assumed no one ever would be able to translate. But a French scholar, Jean Champollion, successively matched, character for character, both the unknown text and the hieroglyphics with the known Greek text, and he offered a **thesis**[6] that the texts read the same. Essentially, he had cracked the mystery of the previously undeciphered hieroglyphics in which much of mankind's earliest history was recorded.

The key that had unlocked a door into the past fascinated me. I seemed to feel it had some special personal significance, but I couldn't imagine what. It was on a plane returning to the United States when an idea hit me. Using language chiseled into stone, the French scholar had deciphered a historic unknown by matching it with that which was known. That presented me a rough **analogy**[7]: In the oral history that Grandma, Aunt Liz, Aunt Plus, Cousin Georgia, and the others had always told on the boyhood Henning front porch, I had an unknown **quotient**[8] in those strange words or sounds passed on by the African. I got to thinking about them: "Kin-tay," he had said, was his name. "*Ko*" he had called a guitar. "Kamby Bolongo" he had called a river in Virginia. They were mostly sharp, angular sounds, with "*k*" predominating. These sounds probably had undergone some changes across the generations of being passed down, yet unquestionably they represented **phonetic**[9] snatches of whatever was the specific tongue spoken by my African ancestor who was a family legend. My plane from London was circling to land at

---

[5] **hieroglyphics**—pictorial symbols used in ancient writing.

[6] **thesis**—proposition.

[7] **analogy**—example of something similar.

[8] **quotient**—element that yields an answer. In mathematics, the quotient is the answer to a division problem.

[9] **phonetic**—of or relating to spoken rather than written language.

New York with me wondering: What specific African tongue was it? Was there any way in the world that maybe I could find out?

*   *   *

Now over thirty years later the sole surviving one of the old ladies who had talked the family narrative on the Henning front porch was the youngest among them, Cousin Georgia Anderson. Grandma was gone, and all of the others too. . . .

I flew to Kansas City again, to see Cousin Georgia.

I think that I will never quite get over her instant response when I raised the subject of the family story. Wrinkled and ailing, she jerked upright in her bed, her excitement like boyhood front-porch echoes:

"Yeah, boy, dat African say his name was 'Kin-tay'! . . . He say de guitar a *'ko,'* de river 'Kamby Bolongo,' an' he was choppin' wood to make hisself a drum when dey cotched 'im!"

Cousin Georgia became so emotionally full of the old family story that Floyd, Bea, and I had a time trying to calm her down. I explained to her that I wanted to try to see if there was any way that I could possibly find where our "Kin-tay" had come from . . . which could reveal *our* ancestral tribe.

"You go 'head, boy!" exclaimed Cousin Georgia. "Yo' sweet grandma an' all of 'em—dey up dere *watchin'* you!"

The thought made me feel something like . . . *My God!*

From Census Rolls to Africa

Soon after, I went to the National Archives in Washington, D.C., and told a reading-room desk attendant that I was interested in Alamance County, North

Carolina, census records just after the Civil War. Rolls of microfilm were delivered. I began turning film through the machine, feeling a mounting sense of intrigue while viewing an endless parade of names recorded in that old-fashioned penmanship of different 1800s census takers. After several of the long microfilm rolls, tiring, suddenly in utter astonishment I found myself looking down there on: "Tom Murray, black, blacksmith—," "Irene Murray, black, housewife—" . . . followed by the names of Grandma's older sisters—most of whom I'd listened to countless times on Grandma's front porch. "Elizabeth, age 6"—nobody in the world but my Great Aunt Liz! At the time of that census, Grandma wasn't even born yet!

It wasn't that I hadn't believed the stories of Grandma and the rest of them. You just *didn't* not believe my grandma. It was simply so uncanny sitting staring at those names actually right there in official U.S. government records.

Then living in New York, I returned to Washington as often as I could manage it—searching in the National Archives, in the Library of Congress, in the Daughters of the American Revolution Library. Wherever I was, whenever black library attendants perceived the nature of my search, documents I'd requested would reach me with a miraculous speed. From one or another source during 1966, I was able to document at least the highlights of the cherished family story; I would have given anything to be able to tell Grandma—then I would remember what Cousin Georgia had said, that she, all of them, were "up there watchin'."

Now the thing was where, what, how could I pursue those strange phonetic sounds that it was always said our African ancestor had spoken. . . .

I had a long talk with George Sims, with whom I'd grown up in Henning, and who is a master researcher. After a few days, George brought me a list of about a dozen people academically renowned for their knowledge of African **linguistics**.[10] One whose background intrigued me quickly was a Belgian, Dr. Jan Vansina. After study at the University of London's School of African and Oriental Studies, he had done his early work living in African villages and written a book called *La Tradition Orale*. I telephoned Dr. Vansina where he now taught at the University of Wisconsin, and he gave me an appointment to see him. It was a Wednesday morning that I flew to Madison, Wisconsin, motivated by my intense curiosity about some strange phonetic sounds . . . and with no dream in this world of what was about to start happening. . . .

That evening in the Vansinas' living room, I told him every syllable I could remember of the family narrative heard since little boyhood—recently buttressed by Cousin Georgia in Kansas City. Dr. Vansina, after listening intently throughout, then began asking me questions. Being an oral historian, he was particularly interested in the physical transmission of the narrative down across generations.

We talked so late that he invited me to spend the night, and the next morning Dr. Vansina, with a very serious expression on his face, said, "I wanted to sleep on it. The **ramifications**[11] of phonetic sounds preserved down across your family's generations can be immense." He said that he had been on the phone with a colleague Africanist, Dr. Philip Curtin; they both felt certain that the sounds I'd conveyed to him were from the "Mandinka" tongue. I'd never heard that word; he told me that it was the language spoken by the Mandingo people. Then he guess-translated certain of the sounds. One of them probably meant cow or cattle; another probably meant the baobab tree, generic in West

---

[10] **linguistics**—the study of the structure of human speech.
[11] **ramifications**—results or consequences.

Africa. The word *ko*, he said, could refer to the *kora*, one of the Mandingo people's oldest stringed instruments, made of a halved large dried gourd covered with goatskin, with a long neck, and twenty-one strings with a bridge. An enslaved Mandingo might relate the *kora* visually to some among the types of stringed instruments that U.S. slaves had.

The most involved sound I had heard and brought was Kamby Bolongo, my ancestor's sound to his daughter Kizzy as he had pointed to the Mattaponi River in Spotsylvania County, Virginia. Dr. Vansina said that without question, bolongo meant, in the Mandinka tongue, a moving water, as a river; preceded by "Kamby," it could indicate the Gambia River.

I'd never heard of it.

An incident happened that would build my feeling —especially as more uncanny things occurred—that, yes, they were up there watchin'. . . .

I was asked to speak at a seminar held at Utica College, Utica, New York. Walking down a hallway with the professor who had invited me, I said I'd just flown in from Washington and why I'd been there. "The Gambia? If I'm not mistaken, someone mentioned recently that an outstanding student from that country is over at Hamilton."

The old, distinguished Hamilton College was maybe a half hour's drive away, in Clinton, New York. Before I could finish asking, a Professor Charles Todd said, "You're talking about Ebou Manga." Consulting a course roster,[12] he told me where I could find him in an agricultural economics class. Ebou Manga was small of build, with careful eyes, a reserved manner, and black as soot. He tentatively confirmed my sounds, clearly startled to have heard me uttering them. Was Mandinka his home tongue? "No, although I am familiar with it." He

---

[12] course roster—list of names of students in a class.

was a Wolof,[13] he said. In his dormitory room, I told him about my quest. We left for The Gambia at the end of the following week.

Arriving in Dakar, Senegal, the next morning, we caught a light plane to small Yundum Airport in The Gambia. In a passenger van, we rode into the capital city of Banjul (then Bathurst). Ebou and his father, Alhaji Manga—Gambians are mostly Moslem—assembled a small group of men knowledgeable in their small country's history, who met with me in the lounge of the Atlantic Hotel. As I had told Dr. Vansina in Wisconsin, I told these men the family narrative that had come down across the generations. . . .

When I had finished, they said almost with wry amusement, "Well, of course 'Kamby Bolongo' would mean Gambia River; anyone would know that." I told them, hotly that no, a great many people *wouldn't* know it! Then they showed a much greater interest that my 1760s ancestor had insisted his name was "Kin-tay." "Our country's oldest villages tend to be named for the families that settled those villages centuries ago," they said. Sending for a map, pointing, they said, "Look, here is the village of Kinte-Kundah. And not too far from it, the village of Kinte-Kundah Jan-neh-Ya."

Then they told me something of which I'd never have dreamed: of very old men, called *griots*, still to be found in the older back-country villages, men who were in effect living, walking archives of oral history. A senior *griot* would be a man usually in his late sixties or early seventies; below him would be progressively younger *griots*—and apprenticing boys, so a boy would be exposed to those *griots'* particular line of narrative for forty or fifty years before he could qualify as a senior *griot*, who told on special occasions the centuries-old histories of villages, of clans, of families, of great

---

[13] Wolof—member of a group of West African people.

heroes. Throughout the whole of black Africa such oral chronicles had been handed down since the time of the ancient forefathers, I was informed, and there were certain legendary *griots* who could narrate **facets**[14] of African history literally for as long as three days without ever repeating themselves.

Seeing how astounded I was, these Gambian men reminded me that every living person ancestrally goes back to some time and some place where no writing existed; and then human memories and mouths and ears were the only ways those human beings could store and relay information. They said that we who live in the Western culture are so conditioned to the "crutch of print" that few among us comprehend what a trained memory is capable of.

Since my forefather had said his name was "Kintay"—properly spelled "Kinte," they said—and since the Kinte clan was old and well known in The Gambia, they promised to do what they could to find a *griot* who might be able to assist my search.

Back in the United States, I began devouring books on African history. It grew quickly into some kind of obsession to correct my ignorance concerning the earth's second-largest continent. It embarrasses me to this day that up to then my images about Africa had been largely derived or inferred from Tarzan movies and my very little authentic knowledge had come from only occasional leafings through the *National Geographic*. All of a sudden now, after reading all day, I'd sit on the edge of my bed at night studying a map of Africa, memorizing the different countries' relative positions and the principal waters where slave ships had operated.

After some weeks, a registered letter came from The Gambia; it suggested that when possible, I should come back. . . .

---

[14] **facets**—aspects, parts.

Success

I again visited Cousin Georgia in Kansas City—
something had urged me to do so, and I found her quite
ill. But she was thrilled to hear both what I had learned
and what I hoped to learn. She wished me Godspeed,
and I flew then to Africa.

The same men with whom I had previously talked
told me now in a rather matter-of-fact manner that they
had caused word to be put out in the back country, and
that a *griot* very knowledgeable of the Kinte clan had
indeed been found—his name, they said, was "Kebba
Kanji Fofana." I was ready to have a fit. "Where *is* he?"
They looked at me oddly: "He's in his village."

I discovered that if I intended to see this *griot*, I was
going to have to do something I'd never have dreamed
I'd ever be doing—organizing what seemed, at least to
me then, a kind of minisafari! It took me three days of
negotiating through unaccustomed endless African
palaver[15] finally to hire a launch to get upriver; to rent a
lorry and a Land Rover to take supplies by a round-
about land route; to hire finally a total of fourteen people,
including three interpreters and four musicians, who
had told me that the old *griots* in the back country
wouldn't talk without music in the background. . . .

There is an expression called "the peak experience"
—that which emotionally, nothing in your life ever tran-
scends. I've had mine, that first day in the back country
of black West Africa.

When we got within sight of Juffure,[16] the children
who were playing outside gave the alert, and the people
came flocking from their huts. It's a village of only about
seventy people. Like most back-country villages, it was
still very much as it was two hundred years ago, with its

---

[15] **palaver**—idle talk, blather; in the African sense, also a discussion or con-
ference to settle a dispute.

[16] Juffure—village where Haley's ancestors apparently lived.

circular mud houses and their conical thatched roofs. Among the people as they gathered was a small man wearing an off-white robe, a pillbox hat over an **aquiline-featured**[17] black face, and about him was an aura of "somebodiness" until I knew he was the man we had come to see and hear.

As the three interpreters left our party to converge upon him, the seventy-odd other villagers gathered closely around me, in a kind of horseshoe pattern, three or four deep all around; had I stuck out my arms, my fingers would have touched the nearest ones on either side. They were all staring at me. Their eyes just raked me. Their foreheads were furrowed with their very intensity of staring. A kind of **visceral**[18] surging or a churning sensation started up deep inside me; bewildered, I was wondering what on earth was this . . . then in a little while it was rather as if some full-gale force of realization rolled in on me: Many times in my life I had been among crowds of people, but never where *every one was jet black!*

Rocked emotionally, my eyes dropped downward as we tend to do when we're uncertain, insecure, and my glance fell upon my own hands' brown complexion. This time more quickly than before, and even harder, another gale-force emotion hit me: I felt myself some variety of a hybrid . . . I felt somehow impure among the pure; it was a terribly shaming feeling. About then, abruptly the old man left the interpreters. The people immediately also left me now to go crowding about him.

One of my interpreters came up quickly and whispered in my ears, "They stare at you so much because they have never here seen a black American." When I grasped the significance, I believe that hit me harder than what had already happened. They hadn't been

---

[17] **aquiline-featured**—having a face with a curved, prominent nose, like an eagle.

[18] **visceral**—relating to the internal organs or guts.

looking at me as an individual, but I represented in their eyes a symbol of the twenty-five millions of us black people whom they had never seen, who lived beyond an ocean . . . .

The old man sat down, facing me, as the people hurriedly gathered behind him. Then he began to recite for me the ancestral history of the Kinte clan, as it had been passed along orally down across centuries from the forefathers' time. It was not merely conversational, but more as if a scroll were being read; for the still, silent villagers, it was clearly a formal occasion. The *griot* would speak, bending forward from the waist, his body rigid, his neck cords standing out, his words seeming almost physical objects. After a sentence or two, seeming to go limp, he would lean back, listening to an interpreter's translation. Spilling from the *griot's* head came an incredibly complex Kinte clan lineage that reached back across many generations: who married whom; who had what children; what children then married whom; then their offspring. It was all just unbelievable. I was struck not only by the profusion of details, but also by the narrative's biblical style, something like: "—and so-and-so took as a wife so-and-so, and begat . . . and begat . . . and begat. . . ." He would next name each begat's eventual spouse, or spouses, and their averagely numerous offspring, and so on. To date things the *griot* linked them to events, such as "—in the year of the big water"—a flood—"he slew a water buffalo." To determine the calendar date, you'd have to find out when that particular flood occurred.

Simplifying to its essence the encyclopedic saga that I was told, the *griot* said that the Kinte clan had begun in the country called Old Mali. Then the Kinte men traditionally were blacksmiths, "who had conquered fire," and the women mostly were potters and weavers. In time, one branch of the clan moved into the country called Mauretania; and it was from Mauretania that one son of this clan, whose name was Kairaba Kunta Kinte—a *marabout*, or holy man of the Moslem faith— journeyed down into the country called The Gambia. He went first to a village called Pakali N'Ding, stayed there for a while, then went to a village called Jiffarong, and then to the village of Juffure.

In Juffure, Kairaba Kunta Kinte took his first wife, a Mandinka maiden whose name was Sireng. And by her he begot two sons, whose names were Janneh and Saloum. Then he took a second wife; her name was Yaisa. And by Yaisa, he begot a son named Omoro.

Those three sons grew up in Juffure until they became of age. Then the elder two, Janneh and Saloum, went away and founded a new village called Kinte-Kundah Janneh-Ya. The youngest son, Omoro, stayed on in Juffure village until he had thirty rains—years—of age, then he took as his wife a Mandinka maiden named Binta Kebba. And by Binta Kebba, roughly between the years 1750 and 1760, Omoro Kinte begat four sons, whose names were, in the order of their birth, Kunta, Lamin, Suwadu, and Madi.

The old *griot* had talked for nearly two hours up to then, and perhaps fifty times the narrative had included some detail about someone whom he had named. Now after he had just named those four sons, again he appended a detail, and the interpreter translated—

"About the time the King's soldiers came"—another of the *griot's* timefixing references—"the eldest of these four sons, Kunta, went away from his village to chop wood . . . and he was never seen again. . . ." And the griot went on with his narrative.

I sat as if I were carved of stone. My blood seemed to have congealed. This man whose lifetime had been in this back-country African village had no way in the world to know that he had just echoed what I had heard all through my boyhood years on my grandma's front porch in Henning, Tennessee . . . of an African who always had insisted that his name was "Kin-tay"; who had called a guitar a "*ko*," and a river within the state of Virginia, "Kamby Bolongo"; and who had been kidnapped into slavery while not far from his village, chopping wood, to make himself a drum.

I managed to fumble from my dufflebag my basic notebook, whose first pages containing grandma's story I showed to an interpreter. After briefly reading, clearly astounded, he spoke rapidly while showing it to the old *griot*, who became agitated; he got up, exclaiming to the people, gesturing at my notebook in the interpreter's hands, and *they* all got agitated.

I don't remember hearing anyone giving an order, I only recall becoming aware that those seventy-odd people had formed a wide human ring around me, moving counterclockwise, chanting softly, loudly, softly; their bodies close together, they were lifting their knees high, stamping up reddish puffs of the dust. . . .

The woman who broke from the moving circle was one of about a dozen whose infant children were within cloth slings across their backs. Her jet-black face deeply contorting, the woman came charging toward me, her bare feet slapping the earth, and snatching her baby free, she thrust it at me almost roughly, the gesture saying "Take it!" . . . and I did, clasping the baby to me. Then she snatched away her baby; and another woman was thrusting her baby, then another, and another . . . until I had embraced probably a dozen babies. I wouldn't learn until maybe a year later, from a Harvard University professor, Dr. Jerome Bruner, a scholar of such matters, "You didn't know you were participating in one of the oldest ceremonies of humankind, called 'The laying on of hands'! In their way, they were telling you 'Through this flesh, which is us, we are you, and you are us!'". . . .

Since we had come by the river, I wanted to return by land. As I sat beside the wiry young Mandingo driver who was leaving dust pluming behind us on the hot, rough, pitted, back-country road toward Banjul, there came from somewhere into my head a staggering awareness . . . that *if* any black American could be so blessed as I had been to know only a few ancestral clues—could he or she know *who* was either the **paternal**[19] or **maternal**[20] African ancestor or ancestors, and about *where* that ancestor lived when taken, and finally about *when* the ancestor was taken—then only those few clues might well see that black American able to locate some **wizened**[21] old black *griot* whose narrative could reveal the black American's ancestral clan, perhaps even the very village. . . .

My mind reeled with it all as we approached another, much larger village. Staring ahead, I realized that word of what had happened in Juffure must have left there well before I did. The driver slowing down, I could see this village's people thronging the road ahead; they were waving, amid their **cacophony**[22] of crying out something; I stood up in the Land Rover, waving back as they seemed grudging to open a path for the Land Rover.

I guess we had moved a third of the way through the village when it suddenly registered in my brain what they were all crying out . . . the wizened, robed elders and younger men, the mothers and the naked tar-black children, they were all waving up at me; their expressions buoyant, beaming, all were crying out together, *"Meester Kinte! Meester Kinte!"*

Let me tell you something: I am a man. A sob hit me somewhere around my ankles; it came surging upward, and flinging my hands over my face, I was just bawling, as I hadn't since I was a baby. *"Meester Kinte!"* I just felt

---

[19] **paternal**—of the father.

[20] **maternal**—of the mother.

[21] **wizened**—shriveled, wrinkled.

[22] **cacophony**—harsh, discordant sounds.

like I was weeping for all of history's incredible atrocities against fellowmen, which seems to be mankind's greatest flaw. . . .

Flying homeward from Dakar, I decided to write a book. My own ancestors' would automatically also be a symbolic saga of all African-descent people—who are without exception the seeds of someone like Kunta who was born and grew up in some black African village, someone who was captured and chained down in one of those slave ships that sailed them across the same ocean, into some succession of plantations, and since then a struggle for freedom.

In New York, my waiting telephone messages included that in a Kansas City Hospital, our eighty-three-year-old Cousin Georgia had died. Later, making a time-zone adjustment, I discovered that she passed away within the very hour that I had walked into Juffure Village. I think that as the last of the old ladies who talked the story on Grandma's front porch, it had been her job to get me to Africa, then she went to join the others up there watchin'.

QUESTIONS TO CONSIDER

1. What do you think motivated Alex Haley to undertake such an exhaustive and expensive search for information about his ancestors? In what ways was his search made especially difficult?

2. What role do *griots* play in Gambian culture? In your opinion, what people or institutions might play the same role in the United States?

3. In what way was *Roots*, in Haley's words, "a buoy to black self-esteem and a reminder of the universal truth that we are all descendants of the same Creator?"

African Roots

Recreating Kunta Kinte's Africa *Inspired by Alex Haley's Roots, author John Devere and photographer Jurgen Vollmer journeyed through western Africa in the late 1970s. They traveled from Juffure, the village from which Kunta Kinte was abducted by slavers, through The Gambia and Senegal to the slave port Dakar, from which so many Africans were shipped to the Americas. Along the way, they documented the land, still largely unchanged, and published their work in* Black Genesis: African Roots.

"Kamby Bolongo" Devere wrote of the luxurious plant growth that crowded the red dirt road to Juffure with tropical foliage and of the swelling streams, or *bolongs*, that empty into the Gambia River.

▲

A Wolof woman works in the garden beside her thatched roof hut, much as Kunta Kinte's kinswomen must have done in his lifetime.

Villagers confer in the shade of a large tree.

The *Griot* Foday Fofana, grandson of Haley's *griot* Kebba Kanji Fofana, strides through his ancestral village.

▼

A Slave Describes His Capture

BY OLAUDAH EQUIANO

An African's life as a slave began with being kidnapped and forcibly removed from home and family. Few first-hand accounts remain of this experience. Among the most eloquent is Olaudah Equiano's story. Published in 1789, Equiano's description of his life was so much admired and widely read that five years after its publication it had run into nine editions. In his book, Equiano tells of his being taken from his people around the year 1750, when he was a child in what is now the country of Nigeria. On board a slave ship, he was transported first to Britain's southern colonies in America, and then to Barbados, where he was eventually able to purchase his own freedom. He settled in England and became an outspoken opponent of slavery, speaking and publishing widely on the topic. His book, The Interesting Narrative of the Life of Olaudah Equiano or Gustavus Vassa, the African, *describes in detail what he saw and felt before, during, and after his life as a slave.*

. . . Our **tillage**[1] is exercised in a large plain or common. . . . This common is often the theater of war, and therefore when our people go out to till their land they not only go in a body but generally take their arms with them for fear of a surprise, and when they **apprehend**[2] an invasion they guard the avenues to their dwellings by driving sticks into the ground, which are so sharp at one end as to pierce the foot and are generally dipped in poison. From what I can recollect of these battles, they appear to have been irruptions of one little state or district on the other to obtain prisoners or booty. Perhaps they were incited to this by those traders who brought the European goods . . . amongst us. Such a mode of obtaining slaves in Africa is common, and I believe more are procured this way and by kidnapping than any other. . . .

. . . I grew up till I was turned the age of 11, when an end was put to my happiness in the following manner. . . . One day, when all our people were gone out to their works as usual and only I and my dear sister were left to mind the house, two men and a woman got over our walls, and in a moment seized us both, and without giving us time to cry out or make resistance they stopped our mouths and ran off with us into the nearest wood. . . . The next day proved a day of greater sorrow than I had yet experienced, for my sister and I were then separated while we lay clasped in each other's arms. It was in vain that we besought them not to part us; she was torn from me and immediately carried away, while I was left in a state of distraction not to be described. I cried and grieved continually, and for several days I did not eat anything but what they forced into my mouth. At length, after many days' traveling, during which I had often changed masters, I got into the hands of a chieftain

---

[1] **tillage**—farmland.

[2] **apprehend**—anticipate.

in a very pleasant country. This man had two wives and some children, and they all used me extremely well and did all they could to comfort me, particularly the first wife, who was something like my mother. Although I was a great many days journey from my father's house, yet these people spoke exactly the same language with us. This first master of mine, as I may call him, was a smith, and my principal employment was working his bellows, which were the same kind as I had seen in my vicinity. . . .

Soon after this my master's only daughter and child by his first wife sickened and died, which affected him so much that for some time he was almost frantic, and really would have killed himself had he not been watched and prevented. However, in a small time afterwards he recovered and I was again sold. I was now carried to the left of the sun's rising, through many different countries and a number of large woods. . . .

From the time I left my own nation I always found somebody that understood me till I came to the sea coast. The languages of different nations did not totally differ, nor were they so **copious**[3] as those of the Europeans, particularly the English. They were therefore easily learned, and while I was journeying thus through Africa I acquired two or three different tongues. . . .

All the nations and people I had hitherto passed through resembled our own in their manner, customs, and language: but I came at length to a country the inhabitants of which differed from us in all those particulars. . . . They cooked also in iron pots and had European cutlasses and crossbows, which were unknown to us, and fought with their fists amongst themselves. Their women were not so modest as ours, for they ate and drank and slept with their men. But above all, I was amazed to see no sacrifices or offerings

---

[3] **copious**—ample, in this case, containing many words.

among them. In some of those places the people ornamented themselves with scars, and likewise filed their teeth very sharp. They wanted sometimes to ornament me in the same manner, but I would not **suffer**[4] them, hoping that I might some time be among a people who did not thus disfigure themselves, as I thought they did. At last I came to the banks of a large river, which was covered with canoes in which the people appeared to live with their household utensils and provisions of all kinds. I was beyond measure astonished at this, as I had never before seen any water larger than a pond or a rivulet: and my surprise was mingled with no small fear when I was put into one of these canoes and we began to paddle and move along the river. . . . Thus I continued to travel, sometimes by land, sometimes by water, through different countries and various nations, till at the end of six or seven months after I had been kidnapped I arrived at the sea coast.

The first object which saluted my eyes when I arrived on the coast was the sea, and a slave ship which was then riding at anchor and waiting for its cargo. These filled me with astonishment, which was soon converted into terror when I was carried on board. I was immediately handled and tossed up[5] to see if I were sound by some of the crew, and I was now persuaded that I had gotten into a world of bad spirits and that they were going to kill me. Their complexions too differing so much from ours, their long hair and the language they spoke (which was very different from any I had ever heard) united to confirm me in this belief. Indeed such were the horrors of my views and fears at the moment that, if ten thousand worlds had been my own, I would have freely parted with them all to have

---

[4] **suffer**—permit.

[5] tossed up—roughly treated.

exchanged my condition with that of the **meanest**[6] slave in my own country. When I looked round the ship too and saw a large furnace or copper boiling and a multitude of black people of every description chained together, every one of their countenances expressing dejection and sorrow, I no longer doubted of my fate; and quite overpowered with horror and anguish, I fell motionless on the deck and fainted. When I recovered a little I found some black people about me, who I believed were some of those who had brought me on board and had been receiving their pay; they talked to me in order to cheer me, but all in vain. I asked them if we were not to be eaten by those white men with horrible looks, red faces, and loose hair. They told me I was not, and one of the crew brought me a small portion of spirituous liquor in a wine glass, but being afraid of him I would not take it out of his hand. One of the blacks therefore took it from him and gave it to me, and I took a little down my palate, which instead of reviving me, as they thought it would, threw me into the greatest consternation at the strange feeling it produced, having never tasted such any liquor before. Soon after this the blacks who brought me on board went off, and left me abandoned to despair.

I now saw myself deprived of all chance of returning to my native country or even the least glimpse of hope of gaining the shore, which I now considered as friendly; and I even wished for my former slavery in preference to my present situation, which was filled with horrors of every kind, still heightened by my ignorance of what I was to undergo. I was not long suffered to indulge my grief; I was soon put down under the decks, and there I received such a salutation in my nostrils as I had never experienced in my life: so that with the loathsomeness of the stench and crying together, I became so sick and

---

[6] **meanest**—lowest in status.

low that I was not able to eat, nor had I the least desire to taste anything. I now wished for the last friend, death, to relieve me; but soon, to my grief, two of the white men offered me eatables, and on my refusing to eat, one of them held me fast by the hands and laid me across I think the **windlass**,[7] and tied my feet while the other flogged me severely. I had never experienced anything of this kind before, and although, not being used to the water, I naturally feared that element the first time I saw it, yet nevertheless could I have got over the nettings I would have jumped over the side, but I could not; and besides, the crew used to watch us very closely who were not chained down to the decks, lest we should leap into the water: and I have seen some of these poor African prisoners most severely cut for attempting to do so, and hourly whipped for not eating. This indeed was often the case with myself. In a little time after, amongst the poor chained men I found some of my own nation, which in a small degree gave ease to my mind. I inquired of these what was to be done with us; they gave me to understand we were to be carried to these white people's country to work for them. I then was a little revived, and thought if it were no worse than working, my situation was not so desperate: but still I feared I should be put to death, the white people looked and acted, as I thought, in so savage a manner; for I had never seen among my people such instances of brutal cruelty, and this not only shewn towards us blacks but also to some of the whites themselves. One white man in particular I saw, when we were permitted to be on deck, flogged so unmercifully with a large rope near the foremast that he died in consequence of it; and they tossed him over the side as they would have done a brute. This made me fear these people the more, and I expected nothing less than to be treated in the same manner. . . .

---

[7] **windlass**—a device for winding up rope.

At last we came in sight of the island of Barbados, at which the whites on board gave a great shout and made many signs of joy to us. We did not know what to think of this, but as the vessel drew nearer we plainly saw the harbor and other ships of different kinds and sizes, and we soon anchored amongst them off Bridgetown. Many merchants and planters now came on board, though it was in the evening. They put us in separate **parcels**[8] and examined us attentively. They also made us jump, and pointed to the land, signifying we were to go there. We thought by this we should be eaten by these ugly men, as they appeared to us; and when soon after we were all put down under the deck again, there was much dread and trembling among us, and nothing but bitter cries to be heard all the night from these apprehensions, insomuch that at last the white people got some old slaves from the land to pacify us. They told us we were not to be eaten but to work, and were soon to go on land where we should see many of our country people. This report eased us much; and sure enough soon after we were landed there came to us Africans of all languages. We were conducted immediately to the merchant's yard, where we were all pent up together like so many sheep in a fold without regard to sex or age. As every object was new to me everything I saw filled me with surprise. What struck me first was that the houses were built with storeys, and in every other respect different from those in Africa: but I was still more astonished on seeing people on horseback. I did not know what this could mean, and indeed I thought these people were full of nothing but magical arts. While I was in this astonishment one of my fellow prisoners spoke to a countryman of his about the horses, who said they

---

[8] **parcels**—lots, as in auctions.

were the same kind they had in their country. I understood them though they were from a distant part of Africa, and I thought it odd I had not seen any horses there; but afterwards when I came to converse with different Africans I found they had many horses amongst them, and much larger than those I then saw. We were not many days in the merchant's custody before we were sold after their usual manner, which is this: On a signal given, (as the beat of a drum) the buyers rush at once into the yard where the slaves are confined, and make choice of that parcel they like best. The noise and clamor with which this is attended and the eagerness visible in the countenances of the buyers serve not a little to increase the apprehensions of the terrified Africans, who may well be supposed to consider them as the ministers of that destruction to which they think themselves devoted. In this manner, without scruple, are relations and friends separated, most of them never to see each other again. I remember in the vessel in which I was brought over, in the men's apartment there were several brothers who, in the sale, were sold in different lots; and it was very moving on this occasion to see and hear their cries at parting. O, ye **nominal**[9] Christians! might not an African ask you, Learned you this from your God who says unto you, Do unto all men as you would men should do unto you? Is it not enough that we are torn from our country and friends to toil for your luxury and lust of gain? Must every tender feeling be likewise sacrificed to your avarice? Are the dearest friends and relations, now rendered more dear by their separation from their kindred, still to be parted from each other and thus prevented from cheering the gloom of slavery with the small comfort of being together and mingling their sufferings and sorrows? Why are parents to lose their children, brothers their sisters, or husbands their wives? Surely this is

---

[9] **nominal**—in name only.

a new refinement in cruelty which, while it has no advantage to atone for it, thus aggravates distress and adds fresh horrors even to the wretchedness of slavery.

QUESTIONS TO CONSIDER

1. What was Equiano doing when he and his sister were captured? From what kind of community were they taken?

2. Why do you think the slaves on board the ship were beaten if they did not eat?

3. Equiano carefully notes the different languages spoken by those he met during his travels, as well as the fact that he was owned by several masters before he was shipped to the Americas. What do his observations imply about the scope and structure of the slave trade during this period?

The Middle Passage

BY DANIEL P. MANNIX
AND MALCOLM COWLEY

The journey of slaves to the Americas is called the middle passage because it formed the middle part of the triangle-shaped trade route slave ships followed across the seas. Ships left their home ports in Europe, sailed to Africa to acquire and load their human freight, crossed the Atlantic to the Americas to sell their cargo, and then returned to Europe. In their book Black Cargoes: A History of the Atlantic Slave Trade, *authors Mannix and Cowley describe how slave traders packed their cargo—slaves—to maximize their profits.*

As soon as an assortment of naked slaves was taken aboard a Guineaman [slave ship], the men were shackled two by two, the right wrist and ankle of one to the left wrist and ankle of another. Then they were sent to the hold or, at the end of the eighteenth century, to the "house" that the sailors had built on deck. The women—usually regarded as fair prey for the sailors— and the children were allowed to wander by day almost anywhere on the vessel, though they spent the night between decks in other rooms than the men. All the slaves were forced to sleep without covering on bare wooden floors, which were often constructed of unplaned boards. In a stormy passage the skin over their elbows might be worn away to the bare bones.

William Bosman says, writing in 1701, "You would really wonder to see how these slaves live on board; for though their number sometimes amounts to six or seven hundred, yet by careful management of our masters of ships"—the Dutch masters, that is—"they are so regulated that it seems incredible: And in this particular our nation exceeds all other Europeans; for as the French, Portuguese and English slave-ships are always foul and stinking; on the contrary ours are for the most part clean and neat." Slavers of every nation insisted that their own vessels were the best in the trade. . . .

There were two schools of thought among the Guinea captains, called the "loose-packers" and the "tight-packers." The former argued that by giving the slaves a little more room, with better food and a certain amount of liberty, they reduced the mortality among them and received a better price for each slave in the West Indies. The tight-packers answered that, although the loss of life might be greater on each of their voyages, so too were the net receipts from a larger cargo. If many of the survivors were weak and **emaciated**,[1] as was often the case, they could be fattened up in a West Indian slave yard before being offered for sale. The argument between the two schools continued as long as the trade itself, but for many years after 1750 the tight-packers were in the ascendant.[2] So great was the profit on each slave landed alive in the West Indies that hardly a captain refrained from loading his vessel to her utmost capacity. The hold of a slaving vessel was usually about five feet high. That seemed like wasted space to the

---

[1] **emaciated**—extremely thin, starving.

[2] in the ascendant—dominant, in control.

Guinea merchants, so they built a shelf or platform in the middle of it, extending six feet from each side of the vessel. When the bottom of the hold was completely covered with flesh, another row of slaves was packed on the platform. If there was as much as six feet of vertical space in the hold, a second platform might be installed above the first, sometimes leaving only twenty inches of headroom for the slaves; they could not sit upright during the whole voyage. The Reverend John Newton[3] writes from personal observation:

> The cargo of a vessel of a hundred tons or a little more is calculated to purchase from 220 to 250 slaves. Their lodging rooms below the deck which are three (for the men, the boys, and the women) besides a place for the sick, are sometimes more than five feet high and sometimes less; and this height is divided toward the middle for the slaves lie in two rows, one above the other, on each side of the ship, close to each other like books upon a shelf. I have known them so close that the shelf would not easily contain one more.

> The poor creatures, thus cramped, are likewise in irons for the most part which makes it difficult for them to turn or move or attempt to rise or to lie down without hurting themselves or each other. Every morning, perhaps, more instances than one are found of the living and the dead fastened together.

---

[3] John Newton (1725–1807), an Englishman, was one of the most remarkable figures of the slavery era. A deserter from the British navy who became the captain of a slave ship, Newton had a sudden realization, during a violent ocean storm in 1748, of the immorality of what he was doing. He attributed his being saved from death and his change of heart to the grace of God. Newton left the sea and was ordained an Anglican priest, spending the rest of his life as an outspoken opponent of slavery. Based on his experience, he wrote one of the world's most famous hymns, *Amazing Grace*.

Dr. Falconbridge stated . . . that "he made the most of the room," in stowing the slaves, "and wedged them in. They had not so much room as a man in his coffin either in length or breadth. When he had to enter the slave deck, he took off his shoes to avoid crushing the slaves as he was forced to crawl over them." Taking off shoes on entering the hold seems to have been a widespread custom among surgeons. Falconbridge "had the marks on his feet where [the slaves] bit and pinched him."

In 1788 Captain Parrey of the Royal Navy was sent to measure such of the slave vessels as were then lying at Liverpool and to make a report to the House of Commons. He discovered that the captains of many slavers possessed a chart showing the dimensions of the ship's half deck, lower deck, hold, platforms, gunroom, orlop,[4] and great cabin, in fact of every crevice into which slaves might be wedged. Miniature black figures were drawn on some of the charts to illustrate the most effective method of packing in the cargo.

On the *Brookes*, which Captain Parrey considered to be typical, every man was allowed a space six feet long by sixteen inches wide (and usually about two feet, seven inches high); every woman, a space five feet, ten inches long by sixteen inches wide; every boy, five feet by fourteen inches; every girl, four feet, six inches by twelve inches. The *Brookes* was a vessel of 320 tons. By the law of 1788 it was permitted to carry 454 slaves, and the chart, which later became famous, showed how and where 451 of them could be stowed away. Captain Parrey failed to see how the captain could find room for three more. Nevertheless, Parliament was told by reliable witnesses, including Dr. Thomas Trotter, formerly

[4] orlop—the lowest deck of a ship.

surgeon of the *Brookes*, that before the new law was passed she had carried 600 slaves on one voyage and 609 on another.

QUESTIONS TO CONSIDER

1. The chart showing how 451 slaves could be fitted on board the *Brookes* left Captain Parrey wondering where the captain could fit even three more slaves. What would have had to be done to fit 609 slaves on that ship?

2. What other businesses can you think of that can maximize profits in ways similar to the techniques used on slave ships?

3. What does the argument of the Guinea captains show you about their attitude toward their cargo?

A Day on a Slaver

BY FREDERICK M. BINDER
AND DAVID M. REIMERS

Having put their engineering skills to work to pack the largest possible number of slaves into their ships, it was still necessary for the slavers to devise a routine for the slaves under their control, so that as many as possible would survive the voyage. It is clear that slavers knew that the conditions on board slave ships produced disease and death for too many slaves. Binder and Reimers describe common practices that slavers used to minimize the effects of the potentially deadly middle passage on their human cargo.

If the weather was clear, they were brought on deck at eight o'clock in the morning. The men were attached by their leg irons to the great chain that ran along the **bulwarks**[1] on both sides of the ship; the women and half-grown boys were allowed to wander at will. About nine o'clock the slaves were served their first meal of the day. If they were from the Windward Coast, the fare consisted of boiled rice, millet, or cornmeal, which

---

[1] **bulwarks**—sides of a ship.

might be cooked with a few lumps of salt beef abstracted from the sailors' rations. If they were from the Bight of Biafra, they were fed stewed yams, but the Congos and the Angolans preferred manioc or plantains.[2] With the food they were all given half a pint of water, served out in a pannikin [a small pan or cup].

After the morning meal came a joyless ceremony called "dancing the slaves." "Those who were in irons," says Dr. Thomas Trotter, surgeon of the *Brookes* in 1783, "were ordered to stand up and make what motions they could, leaving a passage for such as were out of irons to dance around the deck." Dancing was prescribed as a **therapeutic**[3] measure, a specific against suicidal melancholy, and also against **scurvy**[4]—although in the latter case it was a useless torture for men with swollen limbs. While sailors paraded the deck, each with a cat-o'-nine-tails in his right hand, the men slaves "jumped in their irons" until their ankles were bleeding flesh. One sailor told Parliament, "I was employed to dance the men, while another person danced the women." Music was provided by a slave thumping on a broken drum or an upturned kettle, or by an African banjo, if there was one aboard, or perhaps by a sailor with a bagpipe or a fiddle. Slaving captains sometimes advertised for "A person that can play on the Bagpipes, for a Guinea ship." The slaves were also told to sing. Said Dr. Claxton after his voyage in the *Young Hero*, "They sing, but not for their amusement. The captain ordered them to sing, and they sang songs of sorrow. Their sickness, fear of being beaten, their hunger, and the memory of their country, &c, are the usual subjects."

While some of the sailors were dancing the slaves, others were sent below to scrape and swab out the

---

[2] Manioc is a plant with a starchy root, also called cassava. Plantains are very similar to bananas but not sweet and served cooked.

[3] **therapeutic**—good, healthful.

[4] **scurvy**—a disease caused by lack of vitamin C, causing bleeding, swelling, and weakness.

sleeping rooms. It was a sickening task, and it was not well performed unless the captain imposed an iron discipline. James Barbot, Sr., was proud of the discipline maintained on the *Albion-Frigate*. "We were very nice,"[5] he says, "in keeping the places where the slaves lay clean and neat, appointing some of the ship's crew to do that office constantly and thrice a week we perfumed betwixt decks with a quantity of good vinegar in pails, and red-hot iron bullets in them, to expel the bad air, after the place had been well washed and scrubbed with brooms." Captain Hugh Crow, the last legal English slaver, was famous for his housekeeping. "I always took great pains," he says, "to promote the health and comfort of all on board, by proper diet, regularity, exercise, and cleanliness, for I considered that on keeping the ship clean and orderly, which was always my hobby, the success of our voyage mainly depended." Consistently he lost fewer slaves in the middle passage than the other captains, some of whom had the filth in the hold cleaned out only once a week. A few left their slaves to wallow in excrement during the whole Atlantic passage.

At three or four in the afternoon the slaves were fed their second meal, often a repetition of the first. Sometimes, instead of African food, they were given horse beans, the cheapest **provender**[6] from Europe. The beans were boiled to a pulp, then covered with a mixture of palm oil, flour, water, and red pepper, which the sailors called "slabber sauce." Most of the slaves detested horse beans, especially if they were used to eating yams or manioc. Instead of eating the pulp, they would, unless carefully watched, pick it up by handfuls and throw it in each other's faces. That second meal was the end of their day. As soon as it was finished they were sent below, under the guard of sailors charged with stowing them away on their

---

[5] nice—careful, fussy.

[6] **provender**—food.

bare floors and platforms. The tallest men were placed amidships, where the vessel was the widest; the shorter ones were tumbled into the stern. Usually there was only room for them to sleep on their sides, "spoon fashion." Captain William Littleton told Parliament that slaves in the ships on which he sailed might lie on their backs if they wished—"though perhaps," he conceded, "it might be difficult all at the same time."

After stowing their cargo, the sailors climbed out of the hatchway, each clutching his cat-o'-nine-tails: then the hatchway gratings were closed and barred. Sometimes in the night, as the sailors lay on deck and tried to sleep, they heard from below "an howling melancholy noise, expressive of extreme anguish." When Dr. Trotter told his interpreter, a slave woman, to inquire about the cause of the noise, "she discovered it to be owing to their having dreamt they were in their own country, and finding themselves when awake, in the hold of a slave ship.". . .

In squalls or rainy weather, the slaves were never brought on deck. They were served their two meals in the hold, where the air became too thick and poisonous to breathe. Says Dr. Falconbridge, "For the purpose of admitting fresh air, most of the ships in the slave-trade are provided, between the decks, with five or six airports on each side of the ship, of about six inches in length and four in breadth; in addition to which, some few ships, but not one in twenty, have what they denominate[7] wind-sails." These were funnels made of canvas and so placed as to direct a current of air into the hold. "But whenever the sea is rough and the rain heavy," Falconbridge continues, "it becomes necessary to shut these and every other con-veyance by which the air is admitted. . . . The negroes' rooms very soon become intolerably hot. The confined air,

---

[7] denominate—give a name to; call.

rendered **noxious**[8] by the **effluvia**[9] exhaled from their bodies and by being repeatedly breathed, soon produces fevers and **fluxes**[10] which generally carry off great numbers of them."

Dr. Trotter says that when tarpaulins were thrown over the gratings, the slaves would cry, "Kickeraboo, kickeraboo, we are dying, we are dying." "I have known," says Henry Ellison, a sailor before the mast, "in the middle passage, in rains, slaves confined below for some time. I have frequently seen them faint through heat, the steam coming through the gratings, like a furnace."

---

[8] **noxious**—harmful, unhealthy.

[9] **effluvia**—fumes.

[10] **fluxes**—diseases causing diarrhea.

QUESTIONS TO CONSIDER

1. How do you think the slavers would have explained their treatment of their cargo?

2. What were the greatest dangers to the slaves' health in the middle passage?

3. What do you think such treatment would do to people's spirit and to their will to live? How do you explain that there were survivors of this crossing?

The Slave Trade

▲
A slave dealer and his customer in Africa, from a seventeenth-century engraving.

▲
Bringing slaves into the Shaka market.

◀ **The March to the Coast** An early drawing of the "victims of Portuguese slave hunters."

Cutaway sectional views of a slave ship, from an engraving published by J. P. Parke, Philadelphia, 1808.
▼

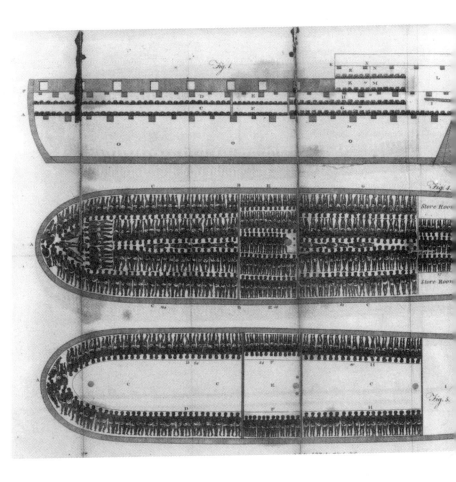

▲

Scene in the hold of the slave ship *Gloria,*
from an engraving by Drake, *Revelation of a
Slave Smuggler, 1858.*

Portrait from the title page from *The
Interesting Narrative of the Life of Olaudah
Equiano, or Gustavus Vassa, the African.* ▶

The slave market in Atlanta, Georgia. Albumen silver stereograph probably by George N. Barnard, 1864.

▲

The Charleston slave sale drawn by Eyre Crowe, secretary to English novelist William M. Thackeray, during his 1856 American trip, for the *Illustrated London News*.

A woodcut, probably from the 1780s, advertises slaves
to be sold on board the ship *Bance-Island*.

Slavery in the Law

The First Africans

BY CHARLES JOHNSON, PATRICIA SMITH,
AND THE WGBH SERIES RESEARCH TEAM

Africans made significant contributions to Britain's developing American colonies. The first black people brought forcibly to what came to be the United States arrived in Jamestown, Virginia, in 1619. However, at that time slavery did not yet exist in the colonies as a legal institution. Africans could eventually gain their freedom—just as indentured white servants. But, as the years passed and colonists prospered, farming larger and larger tracts of land, the treatment of black people changed. As colonists found they needed large amounts of cheap labor to make plantations profitable, they created laws institutionalizing slavery. From that time forward, if you were black you were property, and the slave trade became big business. The following is an account of the life and fortunes of one early black American and his descendants.

> *About the last of August came in a*
> *Dutch man of warre that sold us twenty Negars.*

> —*John Rolfe, Jamestown, 1619*

In the early seventeenth century, the Dutch sought to become major players in the Spanish and Portuguese **maritime**[1] monopoly. They planned and executed well-timed raids on Portuguese ports in Brazil and West Africa and on colonial settlements in Central and South America. And in August 1619, a Dutch ship robbed a Spanish vessel of its cargo—Africans.

The ship emerged as if the violent storm had given it birth, drawing its shape from a clinging mist. Its shimmering edges hardened as it dropped anchor at Jamestown. Those aboard were ghosts before they became men. No one recorded the ship's name or investigated its origins.

The crew offered to trade the Africans for food, and twenty captives were released to their new owners. There had been Africans in North America before, but the first permanent African settlers in an English colony arrived that long-ago summer. It was a full year before the Pilgrims reached Massachusetts on the *Mayflower*.

The blacks who were put to work in Jamestown may have shared the same status as English indentured servants. On that day in 1619, there was probably no difference, no distinction made.

The conditions on early Virginia tobacco plantations were extremely harsh. Field workers were housed in overcrowded shacks and given barely enough food to fuel their work. They had little chance to provide for themselves, for nothing was as important as the efficient production of tobacco.

No one was a slave for life. All the indentured servants worked equally hard and were punished equally.

---

[1] **maritime**—of or relating to seafaring or shipping.

And if they looked far enough into their futures, if the reality of their surroundings had not already destroyed their spirits, they could imagine freedom.

On a March morning in 1622, three years after the mysterious Dutch ship left its human offering at Jamestown, thirty nations of the Powhatan Confederacy[2] sought to avenge the murder of a revered tribal head by waging a full-scale attack on the British. They wanted to push the settlers back into the sea. On the Bennett plantation along the James River, fifty-two colonists lost their lives in the massacre. Among the five survivors was a servant called Antonio.

Antonio may have arrived at the colony from Angola the year before aboard the *James*. Sold into bondage to toil in the tobacco fields, "Antonio, a Negro" is listed as a "servant" in the 1625 census. Virginia had no rules for slaves. So it was possible that Antonio knew hope. Perhaps he felt that redemption was possible, that opportunities existed for him even as a servant. Already, he had done what so many others had failed to do—stay alive.

"Mary, a Negro woman" had sailed to the New World aboard the *Margrett and John*. Soon she became Antonio's wife.

"Antonio, a Negro" became the landowner Anthony Johnson. His history, his motivations, the words he may have spoken, have the same ghostly edges as the mysterious ship that pierced the fog at Jamestown years before. Over the course of a lifetime, he and Mary bought their way out of servitude, raised four children, and struggled to claim a slice of the stubborn new world as their own. Determined to build an independent life, Anthony could not foresee the role his skin color would eventually play in his fate and the fate of his family.

---

[2] Powhatan Confederacy—an alliance among Native American peoples of the northeastern United States.

Although it is not known exactly how or when the Johnsons became free, court records in 1641 indicate that Anthony was master to a black servant, John Casor. During that time, the couple lived on a comfortable but modest estate and Anthony began raising livestock. In 1645, a man identified as "Anthony, the negro" stated in court records, "now I know myne owne ground and I will worke when I please and play when I please."

It cannot be proved that it was actually Anthony Johnson who spoke those words. But if he did not speak them, he felt them, felt them as surely as he felt land beneath his feet. The words didn't reflect his state of ownership as much as they reflected his state of mind. He owned land. He could till the soil whenever he wished and plant whatever he wished, sell the land to someone else, let it lie fallow, walk away from its troubles. He could sit in his house—*his* house—and ignore the land altogether. Anthony Johnson was a man in control of his own.

By 1650, the Johnsons owned 250 acres of land stretched along Pungoteague Creek on the eastern shore of Virginia, acquired through the headright system, which allowed planters to claim acreage for each servant brought to the colony. Anthony claimed five headrights, although there is no way to know if he was actually responsible for the servants' presence in Virginia or if he'd acquired their certificates some other way. Many landowners of the time purchased headrights to increase the size of their claims.

No matter how he amassed his acreage, Anthony's "owne ground" was now **formidable**.[3]

The couple was living a seventeenth-century version of the American dream. Anthony and Mary had no reason not to believe in a system that certainly seemed

---

[3] **formidable**—large, impressive.

to be working for them, a system that equated owner-ship with achievement. If not for the color of their skin, they could have been English.

Very few people who had inked their signatures on indenture forms received the promise of those contracts. At the end of their periods of servitude, many were denied the land they needed to begin their lives again. Anthony Johnson was one of a select few able to consider a piece of the world his own.

The first Virginia colonists thought of themselves as Christians or Englishmen, not white people. The word *white* was not yet used to refer to a type of person. There were owners and servants, and the only thing that made one servant different from another was the contracted length of servitude. If you were a servant, your color did not improve or **exacerbate**[4] that situation. Black and white servants were oppressed equally. They performed the same tasks and were punished in the same way when they were perceived to have failed in some way. White women, later deemed fairest and most fragile, not only worked in the fields alongside black servants, but were also briskly **reprimanded**[5] at the whipping posts.

Sometime in the mid-seventeenth century, that changed. Darker became wrong.

Europeans had long believed that they had the missionary right to enslave anyone who was not a Christian. But slaves could then convert to Christianity and gain their freedom. And since it was impossible to look at a person and determine his or her religious persuasion, physical difference was an easier, more permanent way to exploit the captives. Workers who had reached the end of their indentured period found contracts were not being honored, and the resulting unrest bordered on rebellion.

---

[4] **exacerbate**—aggravate, make worse.

[5] **reprimanded**—punished.

Treating black and white workers differently, making them suspect each other, may have been a swift and easy way to isolate the two factions, smash the budding alliances, and regain control over the workforce. Those in power lived in constant fear that beleaguered black and white laborers would realize strength in numbers and join to rise up against authority. As racial categories grew harsher, the English gradually chose to describe themselves not as Christians, but as white people.

In 1639, the colony of Maryland declared that a Christian baptism did not make a slave free. Religious salvation no longer spelled liberty. Soon the definition of who could be made a slave would change forever. No longer were non-Christians singled out. Now if you did not look European—if your skin was not white—you could be enslaved.

In 1640, three of farmer Hugh Gwyn's servants escaped to Maryland. The circumstances of their "crimes" were identical. When they were captured and carted back to Jamestown for trial, the **disparities**[6] in their punishments mirrored the new **chasm**[7] between black and white.

"The said three servants shall receive the punishment of whipping and to have thirty stripes apiece," the court record stated.

> One called Victor, a Dutchman, the other a Scotchman called James Gregory, shall first serve out their times according to their indentures, and one whole year apiece after . . . and after that . . . to serve the colony for three whole years apiece.
>
> The third being *a negro* named John Punch shall serve his said master or his assigns *for the time of his natural Life.*

---

[6] **disparities**—marked differences.

[7] **chasm**—rift; break.

It was John Punch's physical appearance that sparked the reprimand. In no surviving legal record has any white servant in America been sentenced to spend his life as a slave.

Over time, powerful Virginia landowners began to realize that enslaving Africans made good economic sense. England's economy had revived, and fewer indentured servants were signing up for the voyage to the colony. Colonists saw their life expectancy increase, and "slaves for life" became an attractive investment. No matter how difficult their lives might be, whites were assured that their degradation would never equal that of Africans.

In 1641, Massachusetts became the first English colony in North America to recognize slavery as a legal institution. Connecticut followed in 1650; Virginia in 1661. The impending tragedy now had a heartbeat. In 1663, a Virginia court decided that if a child was born to a slave, that child would also be enslaved.

An African woman could no longer rejoice in the fact that her child would be born free. Because she was black and the child came from her body, the child would serve a master.

There were other options. Blacks and whites could have both retained their indentured status, or both groups could have been doomed to eternal servitude. Standing at the first of many crossroads, the American colonies chose to focus on color difference. The foundation of the agrarian economic system would be the systematic oppression of black people. Once that decision was made, a huge door swung shut. Only the colonies' newest targets of discrimination felt the need to undo what had been done, to set matters back on even ground.

In the relentless march that is history, some changes are instantaneous, lightning swift, extreme enough to change a cultural or physical landscape almost overnight. But the colonies' gradual acceptance of slavery as a race-based economic solution spanned a generation, all the more chilling because there was no one moment to point to and say, "That is where it began." The individuals involved—blacks and whites, landowners and servants—were simply living their lives, day-to-day. And the misfortune of a group of people who were black at the wrong time and place certainly didn't seem to have consequences for the world.

Anthony Johnson symbolized that terrible transformation, that slow turn toward sanctioned oppression. Although he was still free, the proud landowner now wore the face of a slave. In his behavior, he was no different from his neighbors—he worked his land, raised his children, took pride in what he had built. His plantation was the nucleus for one of America's first black communities. But there was nothing he could do about being black.

In 1653, a consuming blaze swept through the Johnson plantation. After the fire, court justices stated that the Johnsons "have bine inhabitants in Virginia above thirty yeares" and were respected for their "hard labor and known service." When the couple requested relief, the court agreed to exempt Mary and the couple's two daughters from county taxation for the rest of their lives. This not only helped Anthony save money to rebuild, it was in direct defiance of a statute that required *all* free Negro men and women to pay taxes.

The following year, white planter Robert Parker secured the freedom of Anthony Johnson's servant John Casor, who had convinced Parker and his brother George that he was an illegally detained indentured servant. Anthony later fought the decision. After lengthy court proceedings, Casor was returned to the Johnson family in 1655.

These two favorable and quite public decisions speak volumes about Anthony's standing in Northhampton County. The very fact that Johnson, a Negro, was allowed to testify in court attests to his position in the community. In the case of the community benevolence following the fire, the fact that Anthony was a Negro never really seemed part of the picture. He was a capable planter, a good neighbor, and a dedicated family man who deserved a break after his fiery misfortune. In the case of his legal battle for Casor, Anthony's vision of property and the value accorded it mirrored that of his white neighbors and the gentlemen of the court. Anthony Johnson had learned to work the system. It was a system that seemed to work for him.

Two years after the Johnson's servant Casor was returned, white planter Matthew Pippen claimed that one hundred acres of the family's land actually belonged to him. It is unclear why the Johnsons failed to contest the claim.

In search of more-yielding land, the Johnsons moved north to Maryland's Somerset County in 1665 after selling two hundred Virginia acres to planters Morris Mathews and John Rowles, on credit. Two years later, influential planter and office holder Edmund Scarburgh delivered 1,344 pounds of tobacco to the Somerset County sheriff, payment due Anthony for the land he'd sold the two planters. . . .

In Maryland, the Johnsons lived on a three-hundred-acre farm called Tonies Vineyard. And in the spring of 1670, Tonies Vineyard was where "Antonio, a Negro"— respected because he had managed to live so long on his own terms—met the end of his life. He was still a free man when the shackles binding him to this world were unlocked.

Upon her husband's death, Mary Johnson renegotiated the lease for ninety-nine years. In August of that year, however, an all-white jury ruled that Anthony's original land in Virginia could be seized by the state "because he was a Negroe and by consequence[8] an alien."[9] The disputed two-hundred-acre parcel was granted to sole occupant John Rowles. And fifty acres that Anthony had given to his son Richard wound up in the hands of wealthy white neighbor George Parker. It didn't matter that Richard, a free man, had lived on the land with his wife and children for five years.

The "hard labor and knowne service" that had served the family so well in the New World was now secondary to the color of their skin. The world that allowed captive slave "Antonio, a Negro," to grow confident as Anthony Johnson, landowner and freeman, ceased to exist. The Virginians no longer needed to lure workers to their plantations. Now they could buy them and chain them there. . . .

---

[8] by consequence—consequently; as a result.

[9] alien—not a citizen.

QUESTIONS TO CONSIDER

1. What differences were there between slaves and indentured servants in the early colonies?

2. In the first part of the seventeenth century, what avenues were open for people of African descent to move from slave to free?

3. What reasons does the author suggest for why skin color became a factor in how workers were treated?

Virginia Slavery Legislation, 1640–1691

Raising tobacco required large numbers of workers for labor in the fields and in the sheds where the leaves were processed for sale. There was a ready market in Europe for the hugely popular, and highly addictive, plant. Tobacco production became increasingly important to Virginia's economy. As more and more Africans found work in the tobacco fields, Virginia's rulers and legislators passed laws to control the black population. The following court decisions and subsequent legislation provide a vivid picture of the management challenges faced by colonial Virginia's tobacco farmers.

[1640] *Whereas Hugh Gwyn* hath . . . Brought back from *Maryland* three servants formerly run away from the said *Gwyn, the court doth therefore order* that the three servants shall receive the punishment of whipping and to have thirty stripes apiece and one called *Victor, a Dutchman,* the other a *Scotchman* called *James Gregory,* shall first serve out their times with their master according to their Indentures, and one whole year apiece after the time of their service is Expired. . . . and after that service to their said master is Expired to serve the colony for three whole years apiece, and that the third being a Negro named *John Punch* shall serve his said master or his assigns for the time of his natural Life here or elsewhere.

[1641] *Whereas . . . John Graweere* being a Negro servant unto *William Evans* was permitted by his said master to keep hogs and make the best benefit thereof to himself provided that the said *Evans* might have half the increase which was accordingly rendered unto him by the said Negro and the other half reserved for his own benefit: And *whereas* the said Negro having a young child of a Negro woman belonging to Lieut. *Robert Sheppard* which he desired should be made a Christian and taught and exercised in the Church of *England*, by reason whereof he the said Negro did for his said child purchase its freedom of Lieut. *Sheppard* with the good liking and consent of *Tho: Gooman's* overseer . . . *the court hath therefore ordered* that the child shall be free from the said *Evans* . . . and remain at the disposing and education of the said *Graweere* and the child's godfather who undertaketh to see it brought up in the Christian religion as aforesaid.

[1661] *Be it enacted* That in case any English servant shall run away in company with any negroes who are incapable of making satisfaction by addition of time, *Be it enacted* that the English so running away in company with them shall serve for the time of the said negroes absence as they are to do for their own by a former act.

[1668] Whereas some doubts, have arisen whether negro women set free were still to be **accompted**[1] **tithable**[2]

---

[1] **accompted**—accounted as, assessed as.

[2] **tithable**—taxable.

according to a former act, *It is declared by this grand assembly* that negro women, though permitted to enjoy their Freedom yet ought not in all respects to be admitted to a full fruition of the exemptions and impunities of England, and are still liable to payment of taxes.

[1669] Whereas the only law in force for the punishment of **refractory**[3] servants resisting their master, mistress or overseer cannot be inflicted upon negroes, nor the obstinancy of many of them by other than violent means supprest, *Be it enacted and declared by this grand assembly,* if any slave resist his master (or other by his master's order correcting him) and by the extremity of the correction should chance to die, that his death shall not be accompted Felony, but the master (or that other person appointed by the master to punish him) be acquit from molestation, since it cannot be presumed that **prepensed**[4] malice (which alone makes murder Felony) should induce any man to destroy his own estate.

[1680] *It is hereby enacted by the authority aforesaid,* that from and after the publication of this law, it shall not be lawful for any negro or other slave to carry or arm himself with any club, staff, gun, sword, or any other weapon of defence or offence, nor to go to depart from his master's ground without a certificate from his master, mistress or overseer, and such permission not to be granted but upon particular and necessary occasions; and every Negro or slave so offending not having a certificate as aforesaid shall be sent to the next[5] **constable**,[6] who is hereby **enjoined**[7] and required to give the said Negro twenty lashes on his bare back well

---

[3] **refractory**—rebellious, unmanageable.

[4] **prepensed**—planned, premeditated.

[5] next—nearest.

[6] **constable**—police officer.

[7] **enjoined**—directed.

laid on, and so sent home to his said master, mistress or overseer. *And it is further enacted by the authority aforesaid* that if any Negro or other slave shall presume to lift up his hand in opposition against any Christian, shall for every such offense, upon due proof made thereof by the oath of the party before a magistrate, have and receive thirty lashes on his bare back well laid on.

[1691] *It is hereby enacted,* that in all such cases upon intelligence[8] of any such Negroes, mulattoes, or other slaves lying out,[9] two of their majesties' justices of the peace of that county, whereof one to be of the **quorum**,[10] where such Negroes, mulattoes or other slave shall be, shall be impowered and commanded, and are hereby impowered and commanded, to issue out their warrants directed to the sheriff of the same county to apprehend such Negroes, mulattoes, and other slaves, which said sheriff is hereby likewise required upon all such occasions to raise such and so many forces from time to time as he shall think convenient and necessary for the effectual apprehending such Negroes, mulattoes and other slaves, and in case any Negroes, mulattoes or other slave or slaves lying out as aforesaid shall resist, run away, or refuse to deliver and surrender him or themselves to any person or persons that shall be by lawful authority employed to apprehend and take such Negroes, mulattoes or other slaves that in such cases it shall and may be lawful for such person and persons to kill and destroy such Negroes, mulattoes, and other slave or slaves by gun or any other ways whatsoever.

---

[8] intelligence—information received.

[9] lying out—being off his or her owner's property, in hiding.

[10] **quorum**—number of members of a legal body that constitute a majority; two magistrates who could issue warrants without the consent, presence, or even the knowledge, of the other.

1. Judging by these laws and court decisions, what do you think frightened legislators most about their black slaves and servants?

2. What was the court's reasoning for its decision permitting a slave owner to go unpunished for beating a slave to death? How does the definition of felony murder in the 1600s compare with today's definition of felony murder?

3. What provisions were made for accurate testimony in the case of assault on a white person by a black one?

A Virginia Planter's Diary

BY WILLIAM BYRD

In England and its colonies in the eighteenth and nineteenth centuries, almost everyone who could read and write kept a diary of the day's events. Many of these diaries have been handed down to us, providing a fascinating picture of daily life in earlier eras. This excerpt from the diary of Virginia plantation owner William Byrd is notable for its portrait of a respectable gentleman of means as he engages in the most cultivated pursuits—reading in Hebrew, Italian, and Greek, the practice of law, dancing, geometry, billiards—and in maintaining household discipline, sometimes with violence and cruelty.

8 FEBRUARY 1709. I rose at 5 o'clock this morning and read a chapter in Hebrew and 200 verses in Homer's Odyssey. I ate milk for breakfast. I said my prayers. Jenny and Eugene were whipped. I danced my dance. I read law in the morning and Italian in the afternoon. . . .

17 APRIL 1709. Anaka was whipped yesterday for stealing the rum and filling the bottle up with water. . . .

10 JUNE 1709. I rose at 5 o'clock this morning but could not read anything because of Captain Keeling, but I played at billiards with him and won half a crown of him and the Doctor. . . . In the evening I took a walk about the plantation. Eugene was whipped for running away and had the **bit**[1] put on him. I said my prayers and had good health, good thoughts, and good humor, thanks be to God Almighty. . . .

3 SEPTEMBER 1709. I read some geometry. We had no court this day. My wife was **indisposed**[2] again but not to much purpose. I ate roast chicken for dinner. In the afternoon I beat Jenny for throwing water on the couch. . . .

1 DECEMBER 1709. I rose at 4 o'clock and read two chapters in Hebrew and some Greek in Cassius. I said my prayers and ate milk for breakfast. I danced my dance. Eugene was whipped again for wetting the bed and Jenny for concealing it. . . .

3 DECEMBER 1709. I rose at 5 o'clock and read two chapters in Hebrew and some Greek in Cassius. I said my prayers and ate milk for breakfast. I danced my dance. Eugene wet the bed again for which I made him drink a pint of it. . . .

27 FEBRUARY 1711. In the evening my wife and little Jenny had a great quarrel in which my wife got the worst but at last by the help of the family Jenny was overcome and soundly whipped. At night I ate some bread and

---

[1] **bit**—metal mouthpiece, usually used for controlling a horse.

[2] **indisposed**—sick.

cheese. I said my prayers and had good health, good thoughts, and good humor, thank God Almighty.

QUESTIONS TO CONSIDER

1. What picture of daily life in Byrd's household do you get from his diary? How does Byrd seem to regard his wife? How old do Jenny and Eugene seem to be? How do they seem to relate to each other?

2. What was most surprising to you about William Byrd's description of his daily life?

3. Note that Byrd reports saying his prayers, and repeatedly thanks God for "good health, good thoughts, and good humor." How do you think Byrd was able to reconcile his treatment of Anaka, Eugene, and Jenny with his religious faith?

Chattels Personal

BY KENNETH M. STAMPP

In other societies, such as Russia in past centuries, many agricultural workers lived in conditions very like slavery. They could not own land, relocate, or disobey orders from a landowner. Nonetheless, Russian peasants were seen as individuals, as persons—they could not be sold, given away, or forced from their homes. This was not the case in America. Historian Kenneth Stampp details how the legal codes of all slave states held that a slave was not to be regarded by law as an individual, but as "chattel" (that is to say, movable personal property). Stampp makes it clear that giving a class of people the legal status of property profoundly affected both slaves and slave owners.

In the customary phraseology of the **antebellum**[1] codes, South Carolina's slaves were "deemed, held, taken, reputed and adjudged in law to be chattels personal, in the hands of their owners and possessors and their **executors**,[2] administrators and **assigns**,[3] to all

---

[1] **antebellum**—before the Civil War.

[2] **executors**—ones appointed to carry out the provisions of a will.

[3] **assigns**—persons to whom property is legally transferred.

intents, constructions and purposes whatsoever." Slaves had the attributes of personal property everywhere, except in Louisiana (and Kentucky before 1852) where they had the attributes of real estate. Neither the laws nor the courts, however, were altogether consistent. In states where slaves were generally considered as personal property, they were treated as **realty**[4] for purposes of inheritance. In Louisiana, where they were supposedly like real property, they retained many of the characteristics of "chattels personal."

Though the slave was property "of a distinctive and **peculiar**[5] character," though recognized as a person, he was legally at the disposal of his master, whose property right was very nearly absolute. "The master," proclaimed the Louisiana code, "may sell him, dispose of his person, his industry, and his labor: he can do nothing, possess nothing, nor acquire anything but what must belong to his master." Even in Kentucky, slaves had "no rights secured to them by the constitution, except of trial by jury in cases of felony."

Legally a **bondsman**[6] was unable to acquire title to property by purchase, gift, or devise; he could not be a party to a contract. No promise of freedom, oral or written, was binding upon his master. According to the Arkansas Supreme Court, "If the master contract . . . that the slave shall be **emancipated**[7] upon his paying to his master a sum of money, or rendering him some stipulated amount of labor, although the slave may pay the money, . . . or perform the labor, yet he cannot compel his master to execute the contract, because both the money and the labor of the slave belong to the master and could constitute no legal consideration for the contract."

---

[4] **realty**—real estate.

[5] **peculiar**—unique, distinctive.

[6] **bondsman**—slave.

[7] **emancipated**—freed from slavery.

Nor could a chattel be a party to a suit,[8] except indirectly when a free person represented him in a suit for freedom. In court he was not a competent[9] witness, except in a case involving another slave. He had no civil rights, no political rights, no claim to his time, no freedom of movement.

Since slaves, as chattels, could not make contracts, marriages between them were not legally binding. "The relation between slaves is essentially different from that of man and wife joined in lawful wedlock," ruled the North Carolina Supreme Court, for "with slaves it may be dissolved at the pleasure of either party, or by the sale of one or both, depending upon the **caprice**[10] or necessity of the owners.". . . No state legislature ever seriously entertained the thought of encroaching upon the master's rights by legalizing slave marriages.

On the contrary, the states guaranteed the rights of property in human chattels in every way feasible.[11] Most southern constitutions prohibited the legislatures from emancipating slaves without both the consent of the owners and the payment of a full equivalent in money. Every state provided severe penalties for the theft of a slave—a common crime in the antebellum South. In Virginia the penalty was two to ten years in the penitentiary, in Tennessee it was five to fifteen years, and in many states it was death.

When a bondsman was executed for a capital crime the state usually compensated the owner, the normal compensation being something less than the full value assessed by a jury. In Arkansas, which gave no compensation, a slaveholder complained bitterly of the "injustice" done him when one of his slaves was hanged

---

[8] suit—lawsuit.

[9] competent—legally recognized.

[10] **caprice**—whim.

[11] in every way feasible—in every way that could be managed or conceived.

for rape. "I had, or ought to have, some claims upon the State for the destruction of my property," he thought. "That would be good policy and good law." Since the execution of a slave resembled the public seizure or condemnation of private property, most of the states recognized the justice of the owner's claim. Sometimes they levied a special tax on slaves and established a separate public fund for this purpose.

There were virtually no restrictions upon the owner's right to deed his bondsmen to others. Normally the courts **nullified**[12] such transfers only if the seller fraudulently **warranted**[13] a slave to be "free from defects" or "vices" such as the "habit of running away." In devising his chattels a **testator**[14] had the power to divide them among his heirs in any way he saw fit—including the power to dissolve families for the purpose of making an equitable distribution. If a master died **intestate**,[15] the division was made in accordance with the state's laws of inheritance.

Sometimes the division provided by a will, or the claims of heirs of a master who died intestate, could not be realized without a sale of slaves. In such cases the southern courts seldom tried to prevent the breaking up of slave families. The executor of an estate was expected to dispose of human chattels, like other property, in the way that was most profitable to the heirs. It may be "harsh" to separate members of families, said the North Carolina Supreme Court, yet "it must be done, if the executor discovers that the interest of the estate requires it; for he is not to indulge his charities at the expense of others."

Advertisements of administrators' sales appeared constantly in southern newspapers. Among several

---

[12] **nullified**—voided.

[13] **warranted**—guaranteed.

[14] **testator**—person leaving a will.

[15] **intestate**—having no will.

dozen in a single issue of a Georgia newspaper were these: "A negro boy, George, about 25 years old," to be sold "for division among the heirs"; two Negro girls, Ann and Lucy, "the former 13, the latter 9 years old," to be sold "for the benefit of the legatees"; fifteen Negroes, "most of them likely[16] and very valuable," to be sold to the highest bidder to settle an estate. Some administrators had to find purchasers for **scores**[17] of slaves. One lot of a hundred, sold "for the benefit of the heirs," included "a large number of healthy fine children, boys and girls, young men and young women, a house carpenter, a plantation blacksmith and a miller; almost every description of servants can be had out of the above negroes."

Since slaves were frequently sold on credit or used as security for loans, they were subject to seizure and sale for the benefit of creditors. A clause in the Virginia code added the **proviso**[18] that human chattels were not to be seized "without the debtor's consent" when there were "other goods and chattels of such debtor for the purpose." Slaves who were seized were to be sold "at the courthouse of the county or corporation, between the hours of ten in the morning and four in the afternoon . . . on the first day of the court." In "execution sales," except for mothers and small children, family ties were ignored whenever it was beneficial to the debtor. As a witness testified before the Georgia Supreme Court, "It is not usual to put up negroes in families at Sheriff's sales."

For several weeks prior to a public auction the sheriff advertised the event in a local newspaper. "Will be sold before the Court-house door in the town of Covington," ran a typical sheriff's notice in Newton County, Georgia, "within the usual hours of sale, on the first Tuesday in February next, the following property,

---

[16] likely—promising.

[17] **scores**—very many. A score is twenty.

[18] **proviso**—condition.

to-wit: Three Negroes—John, a boy about 18 years old; Ann, a girl about 4 years old; Riley, a boy about three years old; all levied on as the property of Burwell Moss, to satisfy a mortgage . . . in favor of Alfred M. Ramsey."

Executors and administrators also sold slaves when it was necessary to satisfy the creditors of the deceased. Their notices of sales "for the purpose of paying debts" against estates appeared in the newspapers alongside the sheriff's notices. Sometimes their advertisements listed bondsmen together with horses, mules, cows, farm implements, and other forms of personal property.

The unsentimental prose of legal codes and court records, of sheriff's notices and administrator's accounts, gave some indication of the dehumanizing effects of reducing people to "chattels personal." Masters who claimed their rights under the laws of property, and who developed the habit of thinking of their chattels in impersonal terms, provided further evidence. The laws, after all, were not abstractions; they were written by practical men who expected them to be applied to real situations. Accordingly, slaves *were* bartered, deeded, devised, pledged, seized, and auctioned. They were awarded as prizes in lotteries and raffles; they were wagered at gaming tables and horse races. They were, in short, property in fact as well as in law.

Men discussed the price of slaves with as much interest as the price of cotton or tobacco. Commenting upon the extraordinarily good prices in 1853, a South Carolina editor reported, "Boys weighing about fifty lbs. can be sold for about five hundred dollars." "It really seems that there is to be no stop to the rise," added a North Carolina editor. "This species of property is at least 30 per cent higher now, (in the dull season of the year), than it was last January. . . . What negroes will bring next January, it is impossible for mortal man to say."

Olmsted noticed how frequently the death of a slave, when mentioned in a southern newspaper, was treated as the loss of a valuable piece of property. A Mississippi editor reported a tragedy on the Mississippi River involving the drowning of six "likely" male slaves "owned by a couple of young men who had bought and paid for them by the sweat of their brows." A young North Carolina planter, who seemed "doomed to misfortune," lost through an accident a slave he had inherited from his grandmother and was thus "minus the whole legacy." One morning James H. Hammond discovered that his slave Anny had "brought forth a dead child." "She has not earned her salt for 4 months[19] past," he grumbled. "Bad luck—my usual luck in this way."

In new regions—for example, in Alabama and Mississippi during the 1830's—the buying and selling of slaves and plantations was the favorite operation of speculators. Everywhere people invested cash in bondsmen as people in an industrial society would invest in stocks and bonds. Affluent parents liked to give slaves to their children as presents. "With us," said a Virginia judge, "nothing is so usual as to advance children by gifts of slaves. They stand with us instead of money." A Kentuckian, "in easy circumstances," was "in the habit of . . . presenting a slave to each of his grandchildren." "I buy . . . Negro boy Jessee," wrote a Tennessee planter, "and send him as a gift to my daughter Eva and the heirs of her body."

Slaveholders kept the courts busy with **litigation**[20] involving titles and charges of fraudulent sales. "The plaintiff declares that the defendant . . . deceitfully represented the . . . slave to be sound except one hip, and a good house servant," ran a typical complaint. A lawyer,

[19] has not earned her salt for 4 months—has not been able to work in the last part of her pregnancy.
[20] **litigation**—court trials.

searching for legal precedents which might justify a claim of "unsoundness" in a slave recently sold, cited past judicial opinions "as regards horseflesh." Two South Carolinians presented to the state Court of Appeals the question of whether the seller or buyer must suffer the loss of a slave who had committed suicide during the course of the transaction. Families were sometimes rent asunder[21] as relatives fought for years, in court and out, over claims to bondsmen.

Litigation between slaveholders and their creditors also brought much business to the southern courts. Many masters who would have refused to sell bondsmen to traders nevertheless mortgaged them and thus often made sales inevitable when their estates were settled, if not before. A Tennesseean with "heavy debts over him" escaped the sheriff by fleeing to Texas with his slaves. This was a familiar story in the Old South, so familiar that the phrase "gone to Texas" was applied to any debtor who fled from his creditors. A slaveholder would abandon his lands and escape in the night with his movable chattels. The courts heard case after case like that of a Georgian who "**clandestinely**[22] removed his property, consisting of negroes, to . . . Alabama, . . . to avoid the payment of his debts," and of a Mississippian, who "ran off . . . into Texas, certain negro slaves, with a view of defrauding his creditors."

The reduction of bondsmen to mere pawns in disputes over titles and in actions by creditors was a **sordid**[23] business. But the suits for trespass masters brought against those who had injured their chattels were no less depressing. For example, when a Kentucky bondsman "died in consequence of injuries inflicted on him by

---

[21] rent asunder—torn apart.

[22] **clandestinely**—secretly.

[23] **sordid**—vile, disgusting.

Thos. Kennedy and others," the owner sued and recovered a judgment for one hundred and ninety-five dollars and costs. A Tennessee slave was hired to a man who permitted him to die of neglect. An indignant judge affirmed that "the hirer of a slave should be taught . . . that more is required of him than to **exact**[24] from the slave the greatest amount of service, with the least degree of attention to his comfort, health, or even life"—and gave a judgment of five hundred dollars for the master, the sole penalty. An Alabama slave was scarred by severe whippings inflicted by his hirer. The owner brought suit on the ground that the slave's "market value . . . was permanently injured."

In all these ways the slave as property clearly had priority over the slave as a person. Contrary to tradition, this was equally the case when masters executed their last wills and testaments. To be sure, some exhibited tender **solicitude**[25] for their "people" and made special provisions for them, but they were decidedly **exceptional**.[26] In addition to those who died intestate and thus left the fate of their slaves to be settled by the courts, most testators—Virginians as well as Mississippians, large as well as small—merely explained how they wished their chattels to be divided among the heirs.

John Ensor, of Baltimore County, Maryland, who died in 1831, bequeathed to a daughter "three negroes . . . also one gray mare and one cow." He gave a second daughter "one negro boy called Lee, one horse called Tom, and one cow." Ensor's will made no further reference to his slaves.

---

[24] **exact**—take.

[25] **solicitude**—concern, care.

[26] **exceptional**—unusual.

QUESTIONS TO CONSIDER

1. Why would American slaves' status as property make any efforts they made to free themselves or act on their own behalf nearly impossible?

2. How did John Ensor, even though he willed his slaves to his heirs, guarantee that some or all of these slaves would have to be sold away from their homes and families? Do you think the slave owner did this purposely or unintentionally?

3. What rights by law did whites have at this time that were denied to slaves?

Resistance
and Rebellion

three

Fighting for Britain in the American Revolution

BY CHARLES JOHNSON, PATRICIA SMITH, AND THE WGBH SERIES RESEARCH TEAM

African Americans resisted slavery and rebelled against it from the very beginning. Some threw themselves overboard from the slave ships. Others repeatedly ran away, in spite of cruel punishments for doing so. The American Revolution brought new opportunities to escape slavery. African Americans fought on both sides of the war. Lord Dunmore, the British governor of Virginia, noticing that "negroes are double the number of white people in this colony," issued a proclamation offering freedom to all who joined His Majesty's troops. And by 1778, when the war was not going well for the Americans, General George Washington accepted black soldiers into the Continental Army, with promises of freedom if they should win. By war's end, about 5,000 black soldiers had fought for the Americans. Thousands more had gone over to the British side. So, when the Americans won the battle of Yorktown in 1781, ensuring them victory in the war, there was widespread alarm among those who had served with the British. The following account, from Africans in America, *tells what happened next.*

George Washington captured two of his escaped slaves after the battle. And the Americans posted guards along the beach to keep fugitive slaves from escaping with the British. "Many Negroes and **mulattos**[1] have concealed themselves on board the ships in the harbor. Others have attempted to **impose**[2] themselves as freemen to make their escape," said Washington. "In order to prevent their succeeding . . . such Negroes are to be delivered to the guards which will be established for their reception."

The British had lost a southern stronghold, but the war continued. Additional British forces and their loyal supporters rapidly retreated toward the coast.

As the battlers for the crown moved across the South to the seaports, thousands of escaped slaves clung to them. They fought to gain passage on ships headed for New York City, where there was still forlorn hope that the British might somehow emerge victorious. Hoping to recover their property, many southern slaveholders traveled north and waited to lay claim to slaves who had fled to fight for the crown and their freedom.

On November 30, 1782, diplomats from Britain and America signed a **provisional**[3] treaty granting full independence to the former colonies. A petulant British delegation refused to sit for the official portrait. The strict, overbearing parents were finally letting the children go. But they weren't happy about it.

Henry Laurens, a retired South Carolina slave trader turned diplomat, was the American negotiator. His friend and former partner Robert Oswald negotiated for the British. Although Laurens was no longer in the business of trading slaves, and in fact had expressed **reservations**[4] about it, he was first and foremost a businessman. He

---

[1] **mulattos**—individuals of mixed racial heritage.

[2] **impose**—force.

[3] **provisional**—temporary.

[4] **reservations**—objections, concerns.

believed that landowners would "need" slaves to rebuild regions torn apart by the war, and he insisted that the British could not leave the United States with property that had not been properly purchased. That included cattle, ammunition, and Negroes.

> His Britannic Majesty shall with all convenient speed and without Causing any destruction or carrying away any Negroes or other property from the American inhabitants, withdraw all his Armies.
> —Provisional Peace Treaty, Article Seven

All former slaves, even those who had spent three or four years living among the English, were to be returned to their masters.

"Peace was restored between America and Great Britain, which **diffused**[5] universal joy among all parties except us," said Boston King.[6]

> [A] report prevailed that all the slaves were to be delivered up to their masters. This dreadful rumor filled us all with inexpressible anguish and terror especially when we saw our old masters coming from Virginia, North Carolina and other parts and seizing upon their slaves in the streets of New York, or even dragging them out of their beds.

Thousands of African Americans like Boston King had chosen to fight with the British. The most desperate elements of the **vanquished**[7] forces crowded Manhattan, realizing that only a chosen few would actually make

---

[5] **diffused**—spread.

[6] Boston King—a hard-working, religious man who had run away from his owner and had fought with the British.

[7] **vanquished**—defeated.

the trip to Britain. There was no way to know who was going to go and who would remain behind to face the wrath of their former owners.

It was George Washington's job to obtain the delivery of all escaped slaves and other property in British possession. But Sir Guy Carleton, the acting British commander, refused to cooperate. In a May 6 meeting with Washington, he declared that his government couldn't possibly ignore the debt owed to Negroes who had fought for the crown. To deliver them into American hands, where they would be punished or returned to slavery, would be, "a dishonorable Violation of the public Faith." Carleton declared that refugees who had joined the British before the November 30 peace treaty would be free, and those arriving after that date would be returned to their owners.

However, Carleton added, if the continued evacuation of the blacks was indeed a break with the treaty, the British would see that owners were compensated for their slaves.

Washington was deeply disturbed by Carleton's proposal. But despite his reservations, the discussion ended with Carleton unflinching in his determination. Washington concluded that the slaves who had escaped from their masters would never be recovered.

Brigadier General Samuel Birch, the commandant of the city of New York under British occupation, was charged with creating a process to **ascertain**[8] which blacks had fought for the crown prior to the treaty and were therefore free to depart with the fleet.

He decided to issue formal certificates to prove length of service with British forces. The treasured certificates would serve as passage aboard a British ship. But, of course, the pieces of paper meant much, much more to those who bargained their lives for a chance at

---

[8] **ascertain**—discover, find out.

freedom. Thousands lined up to plead their cases to a few British officers. They simply had to get themselves, their families, on board.

To quiet former colonists' resistance to the process, Birch also created a commission and devised a list of everyone to whom he issued a certificate. The list, which could also be used to aid in any further arbitration over lost property, became known as *The Book of Negroes*. It was a list of every man, woman, and child who could prove their length of time with the British. Every Wednesday afternoon between May and November 1783, the book was opened in a tavern packed with slaves wishing to prove their qualifications for freedom and owners petitioning for the return of their human property.

> Fine boy, stout wench, blind and lame, nearly worn out, ordinary wench, stout woman, ordinary child, stout man. . . .
> —Descriptions from *The Book of Negroes*

Among the three thousand names listed in the book is that of twenty-three-year-old Boston King, "stout fellow" and former property of Richard Waring of Charleston, South Carolina. King had been a part of the British forces for four years and had invaded North Carolina with Cornwallis.

After the campaigns in South Carolina, Boston King went to Charleston; when the British surrendered that city, he was then taken to New York on one of their warships. Since he was too poor to buy tools, he was unable to practice carpentry. With thousands of other black refugees, he lived in crammed barracks and did odd jobs to support himself. While in New York, he married Violet, a woman of African and Native American descent. In *The Book of Negroes*, she is Violet

King, thirty-five, "stout wench" of Wilmington, North Carolina.

To earn extra money, King worked on a pilot boat. On one **excursion**,[9] he was abducted by an American rebel and sold back into slavery in New Jersey. His new master treated him well, but King burned for freedom:

> [I]ndeed the slaves about Baltimore, Philadelphia and New York have as good **victuals**[10] as many of the English; for they have meat once a day, and milk for breakfast and supper; and what is better than all, many of the masters send their slaves to school at night, that they may learn to read the scriptures. This is a privilege indeed. But alas, all these enjoyments could not satisfy me without liberty.

King later managed to escape and return to New York and Violet.

Now the couple faced a freedom they had never known. Their futures were **tumultuous**,[11] uncertain. Climbing aboard *L'Abondance* in New York harbor, there was no way of knowing what fortune awaited on the other end of the voyage. On board was the Black Brigade—escaped slaves and free blacks who had fought for the British during the Revolutionary War—the last of an estimated four thousand black refugees fleeing servitude.

With 408 other passengers, Boston and Violet King sailed from New York to Port Roseway in Nova Scotia.[12] Those aboard *L'Abondance* formed the community of

---

[9] **excursion**—trip, voyage.

[10] **victuals**—food.

[11] **tumultuous**—filled with violent upheavals.

[12] Nova Scotia—a British colony in what is now Canada.

Birchtown, named in honor of the man who had graced them with the **coveted**[13] certificates to freedom.

In his new home, Boston King began to focus on his relationship with the Lord. He attended prayer meetings and mused over the salvation of his soul:

> I thought I was not worthy to be among the people of GOD, nor even to dwell in my own houses, but was fit only to reside among the beasts of the forest. This drove me out into the woods, when the snow lay upon the ground three or four feet deep, with a blanket, and a firebrand in my hand. I cut the boughs of the spruce tree and kindled a fire. In this lonely situation I frequently entreated the Lord for mercy—but in vain.

One Sunday in March, on his way to service, King "thought I heard a voice saying to me, 'Peace be unto thee!' . . . All my doubts and fears vanished away: I saw, by faith, heaven opened to my view, and Christ and his holy angels rejoicing over me."

Following his religious transformation, King became obsessed with helping others achieve the same state of spiritual well-being. He visited his neighbors and preached during prayer meetings. Then, in 1787, "I found my mind drawn out to **commiserate**[14] my poor brethren in Africa, and especially when I considered that we have the happiness of being brought up in a Christian land. . . ."

King got his wish. Eventually he boarded a ship to Sierra Leone[15] in a journey arranged by the Sierra Leone Company, which was incorporated to **barter**[16] on the African continent. The company also sought to reestablish

---

[13] **coveted**—much desired.

[14] **commiserate**—empathize with; feel concern for.

[15] Sierra Leone—a country on the west coast of Africa.

[16] **barter**—trade.

former slaves in Africa to show that they could govern and support themselves. Boston King was going to introduce his God to brothers and sisters he'd never seen.

He had fought for the British and finally achieved what he'd been promised so long ago. His body was free. Now so was his soul.

By the end of the American Revolution, 100,000 slaves had escaped bondage. Close to twenty thousand left with the British military while others fled in private vessels. Some returned to Africa. Thousands who begged their way aboard the ships lost their freedom anyway. Some wound up as slaves in the Caribbean, trading one misery for another.

The future of those still on American soil was as uncertain as the future of those whose precious certificates had granted them new lives. Their scarred, broken new country failed to embrace them.

QUESTIONS TO CONSIDER

1. How do you think the former slaves would have been able to prove to the commission that they had served with the British army?

2. Aside from religious reasons like those of Boston King, what do you think motivated the black soldiers who had fought for the British to go to Sierra Leone, in Africa, a place that King and most of the others had never seen?

3. What was the conflict between General George Washington and Sir Guy Carleton? What interests was each trying to represent?

Runaways and Punishment

BY EDWARD BALL

*The runaway was an especially hated figure by slave owners.
A successful runaway not only deprived his owner of his or her
"property," but also encouraged other slaves to seek freedom. Every
official therefore had unlimited powers to find and seize suspected
runaways. Slaves who were recaptured were punished in a manner
intended not only to keep the runaway from trying again but also
to frighten other slaves from even thinking of escape. Edward Ball,
a descendant of South Carolina slave owners, felt that "the slave
business was a crime that had not fully been acknowledged. . . ."
In his book* Slaves in the Family, *he recorded his search for his
family's history, which brought him face to face with his own
African-American cousins. What he found in the Ball family's
plantation records and in evidence from newspapers of the period
was sobering. His ancestors harshly punished slaves who ran away
and were recaptured.*

Shortly after he came into his inheritance, Second Elias[1] placed the following advertisement in the *South Carolina Gazette*:

> Run away from my plantation . . . a middle sized negro man, named Carolina, has the mark of a large wound on one of his arms . . . and is well known in and about Charles Town, where he was for some years a fisherman. Whoever takes up and delivers him to Austin and Laurens in Charles-Town, or to me at my plantation . . . shall have Five Pounds reward . . . Elias Ball.

Carolina and his companion, a woman named Patra, had an eleven-year-old son, Truman. To judge from the number of advertisements the Balls placed in newspapers, Carolina was only one of many slaves who tried to escape, often walking off in the night. To flee the plantation was a **treacherous**[2] business, and had been since the start of the colony, long before 1690, when treatments for runaways were encoded in South Carolina law. A chronicle of sorts of the people who tried to escape captivity, and what happened to them, can be put together merely by reading contemporary newspapers.

Carolina, the fisherman who took off, was a veteran in **defiance**.[3] In 1749 he had been jailed and questioned for conspiring with other slaves on the Cooper River to rise up against the rice planters, and he was lucky to get away with his life. When he ran from Second Elias, however, Carolina did not get far; a year after his escape, plantation records show him back on the farm.

Carolina may have gotten "the mark of a large wound on one of his arms" while **plying**[4] his fishing

---

[1] Second Elias—son of the first slave-owning ancestor in Ball's family.

[2] **treacherous**—dangerous.

[3] **defiance**—bold resistance to authority.

[4] **plying**—working at.

trade, but more likely it came from a beating laid on by Second Elias or one of his overseers. Lashings with the cat-o'-nine-tails, beatings with sticks, and burnings of flesh all left tracks that Second Elias and his peers advertised as "distinguishing marks." Carolina was not the only slave of Second Elias who had been beaten enough to leave scars. In October 1766, Mr. Ball placed this ad: "Run Away from my plantation . . . Three New Negro Fellows named Primus, Caesar, and Boson [Boatswain]. . . . Primus is a pretty tall fellow, and has a large scar on one of his shoulders."

The *Gazette* gave the Balls a place to cast the net[5] after the escape of their workers. Advertisements for runaways usually appeared with a picture, an image of a black man running, carrying a spear. More people tried to escape in South Carolina than anywhere else in colonial America, twice as many as fled in the two other major slave provinces, Virginia and Maryland. It may have been that bondage in South Carolina was simply more violent than that farther north. Based on the number of ads, more women tried to flee the rice plantations than the more northern tobacco farms— one of four of the total. But finally, neither sex nor geography could predict who would make off; evidently the childhood memories of those who escaped had more to do with their behavior. More than six out of ten runaways from the Balls and their **peers**[6] had been born in Africa.

One February, Second Elias ran the following announcement in the local paper:

> Run away . . . two young Negro fellows, one this country born, named Tom, a middling tall fellow, has one of his toes cut off; the other is a fellow of the Guiney [Guinea] country,

---

[5] cast the net—look for information.

[6] **peers**—equals, contemporaries.

something shorter than Tom, of a black complexion, named Jemmy . . . a reward of ten pounds for Tom, and five pounds for Jemmy, on delivery of them.

Like Carolina, Tom with the missing toe was evidently from a rebellious family. Young Tom's mother was a field hand named Julatta, and his father was Tom White, the Angolan arrested in the alleged uprising scheme of 1748. By custom, Tom Jr. would have gone in the rice fields when he turned twelve, so that when he escaped, at age twenty-six, he had likely been working thirteen years. After he took off, young Tom disappears from plantation records. He may have either died or, unlike the majority who fled, gotten away for good.

Runaways often fled, were brought back and punished, then left again. In Second Elias's day, some slave owners may have continued to advocate castration—the penalty for repeated escape that dated from the pioneer days—though few masters actually admitted to the practice by writing it down. In a more common punishment, ears and toes were severed (though not hands, required for work). Young Tom's missing toe, mentioned in the paper, may have indicated a previous escape attempt.

The thought that Second Elias Ball practiced amputation on his workers is supported by other evidence from the days of his father. One year, when Red Cap[7] was still alive, the *South Carolina Gazette* ran an ad stating that a slave named Booba had just been captured and waited in jail in Charleston. He "says he belongs to Mr. Ball," the paper said, meaning Red Cap. After listing the man's clothes, the *Gazette* ended its description this way: "Two Toes upon each Foot seem as if they were cut off."

---

[7] Red Cap—the first Elias Ball, nicknamed by his ancestors because in his portrait he is shown wearing a red wool cap.

QUESTIONS TO CONSIDER

1. Why, other than as punishment, might it have been useful to slave owners to have their slaves scarred, branded, or their toes removed?

2. Why does the author think it is significant that a majority of runaways had been born in Africa?

3. Ball mentions a slave who when recaptured was found to have had two toes cut off. What does this tell about the slave's history?

Slave Revolts

Resistance to slavery was not limited to individual runaways. Planned, armed rebellions by slaves took place regularly enough to deeply frighten the white population. Below are three excerpts. The first is an eyewitness account of the Stono Rebellion in South Carolina in 1740. Next is an analysis of the widespread reaction among whites hundreds of miles away in New York City. Their terror could only be calmed by a blood-bath of slaves and imagined collaborators. Lastly, historian William Loren Katz summarizes some of the major slave uprisings of the nineteenth century: Prosser's Plot, the Denmark Vesy Plot, the Nat Turner Rebellion, and the mutinies on the Amistad and Creole.

The Stono Rebellion, 1740
by A Southern White Eyewitness

. . . A number of Negroes having assembled together at Stono, first surprised and killed two young men in a warehouse, and then plundered it of guns and ammunition. Being thus provided with arms, they elected one of their number captain, and agreed to follow him, marching towards the south-west, with colors flying and drums beating, like a disciplined **company**.[1] *. . . they plundered and burnt every house, killing every white person they found in them, and **compelling**[2] the Negroes to join them.*

Governor Bull returning to Charleston from the southward, met them, and observing them armed, spread the alarm, which soon reached the Presbyterian Church at Wiltown. . . . By a law of the province, all Planters were obliged to carry their arms to Church, which at this critical **juncture**[3] proved a very useful and necessary regulation. The women were left in Church trembling with fear, while the militia, under the command of Captain Bee, marched in quest of the Negroes, who by this time had become **formidable**,[4] from the number [of slaves] that joined them.

They had marched about twelve miles, and *spread desolation*[5] *through all the plantations in their way.* They halted in an open field, and began to sing and dance, by way of triumph. During these rejoicings, the militia discovered them. . . . One party advanced into the open field and attacked them, and, having killed some Negroes, the remainder took to the woods and **dispersed**.[6] Many ran back to their plantations, in hopes of escaping suspicion from the absence of their masters; *but the greater part were taken and tried.* Such as had been compelled to join them, contrary to their inclination, were pardoned, but all the chosen leaders and first **insurgents**[7] suffered death.

---

[1] **company**—military unit.

[2] *compelling*—forcing.

[3] **juncture**—point in time.

[4] **formidable**—frightening, impressive.

[5] *desolation*—havoc, destruction.

[6] **dispersed**—scattered.

[7] **insurgents**—invaders, rebels.

The New York City Panic, 1741

by Charles Johnson, Patricia Smith,
and the WGBH Research Team

When colonists in New York heard of the massacre at Stono, their hearts pounded. They knew that it was only a matter of time until their own city erupted. New York City at that time housed the second-largest urban population of Africans in the English colonies. The southern tip of Manhattan Island was home to eleven thousand people, and one in five was enslaved. Only Charleston had a denser slave population.

This was a consequence of the city's direct, almost casual, trade with the West Indies; New Yorkers provided foodstuffs in exchange for slaves from the Caribbean. These slaves were a convenience, not a necessity, and were used primarily for domestic service. Packed into New York City's three square miles, enslaved women, consistently the largest segment of the city's black population, were employed as household servants; African men worked as manservants, stable hands, or drivers, or sometimes as assistants to craftsmen or merchants.

There had been trouble before. In April 1712 in the colony of New York, rebellious slaves torched a building. As the fire raged and spread, enslaved Africans and Indians lay in wait for the whites who came out to extinguish the flames. Before the melee subsided, at least nine white men lost their lives—shot, stabbed, or beaten to death. It was the slaveholder's nightmare, painted in too-vivid colors on the streets of a colonial town.

So white New Yorkers had reason to fear the slaves; they slept warily because of their presence. They imagined the streets running scarlet with the blood of the privileged. Now they believed a larger, more violent uprising was imminent.

The whites in New York were troubled by the strength of young black men, their numbers, their shared language. They were intimidated by the men's tiny rebellions, how they somehow avoided many of the laws meant to control them. Although the law dictated that slaves were not supposed to be on the streets after sunset, possess money, or gather in numbers greater than three, every night those laws were broken publicly. Control was lax and loosely enforced, granting the slaves a treasured degree of independence.

Many other factors fueled the fear in New York. With England at war with Spain, it would take a fleet of Spanish warships approximately ten days to reach the city from Florida. To the north of New York, the French could cross the Canadian border and invade at any time. In the winter of 1740, New York City was an absolutely miserable place.

The cold siphoned the spirit. Food and firewood were running out. Grain prices had spiraled out of control. A special fund designated for the poor was exhausted. And rumor had it that discontented slaves planned to poison the water. New Yorkers didn't wonder *if* disaster would come. They just wondered when.

It came on the eighteenth of March 1741.

The first building to burn was the governor's residence in Fort George, on the southernmost tip of Manhattan Island. It was also the main military barracks. By the middle of the afternoon, it was nothing more than ash and rubble. The following week, another fire broke out, followed by more than a dozen in the next three weeks. This was no small concern, since New York City, like all colonial towns, was a settlement of wooden structures.

Townspeople suspected arson. They believed that perhaps slaves were setting the fires as an act of revenge or as preface to a larger rebellion. Van Sant's warehouse burned. Gergereau's cow stable. The home of Agnes Hilton. A haystack on Joseph Murray's property.

One particular fire adjoined a residence where a slave lived who belonged to a group known as the

Spanish Negroes, sailors who'd been captured aboard a Spanish sloop and sold into slavery while their white shipmates were jailed as prisoners of war. In a petition, the black sailors had threatened to burn the place down if they weren't set free. So after a fire began next door to one of them, all were rounded up and imprisoned.

Soon after, a black man named Cuff Philipse was seen running from another fire, a sure sign for many that the long-feared Negro uprising had begun. In response, almost every African-American male over sixteen was hunted down and locked in the city jail. It was time to find out who was at the heart of this wretched insurrection. Punishment had to be swift and sure.

The official investigation was headed by Daniel Horsmanden, a chief court justice in colonial New York. The main witness, sixteen-year-old white indentured servant Mary Burton, worked for tavern and brothel proprietor John Hughson. Hughson's business regularly catered to black customers, in direct violation of the law.

Mary Burton, inspired by a promise of freedom and a payoff of one hundred English pounds, talked. By the time she finished, thirteen blacks had been burned at the stake, eighteen had been hanged, and more than seventy had been banished to the West Indies, Newfoundland, Suriname, and Spain. Mary Burton implicated every black brought into Horsmanden's courtroom, as well as four whites who were also sent to the gallows.

She testified against the slaves Caesar and Prince, who were hanged for the crime of burglary. Cuff and Roosevelt's Quack, convicted of arson and conspiracy, were granted a stay of execution, but a **rabid**,[8] vengeful mob forced the authorities to kill them anyway. Then Mary Burton testified that her employer, John Hughson, and a prostitute named Peggy Carey were in alliance with the Negroes in their plot to kill every white inhabitant of

[8] **rabid**—violent; raging.

the city. Hughson; his wife, Sarah; and Peggy Carey were hanged. Hughson's daughter Sarah escaped the same fate by joining Mary Burton to spew **allegations**.[9]

On July 1, 1741, convinced solely by the highly questionable testimony of Mary Burton, Judge Horsmanden convicted five of the Spanish Negroes. All five were hanged. Other dead and banished included Antonio, Cuba, Cuffee, Africa, Diego, London, Sussex, Jamaica, Quamino, [and] Othello. Burton then accused English schoolteacher John Ury of being a Jesuit[10] priest in disguise and urging the slaves to violence. On the twenty-ninth of August, Ury was hanged.

The **travesty**[11] came to an end only when Mary Burton began accusing influential, moneyed New Yorkers. She was then hurriedly paid a hundred pounds, freed from her indenture, and, probably, urged to relocate immediately.

An unknown writer beseeched Dr. Cadwallader Colden of New York's Governor's Council in a letter dated June 23, 1741:

> [Sir] . . . the horrible executions among you . . . puts me in mind of our New England witchcraft in the year 1692. . . . I am humbly of the opinion that such confessions . . . are not worth a straw; for many times they are obtained by foul means, by force or torment . . . or in hopes of a longer time to live. . . . I entreat you not to go on . . . making bonfires of the negros and . . . loading yourselves with greater guilt than theirs. For we have too much reason to fear that the Divine vengeance does and will pursue us for our ill treatment to the bodies and souls of our poor slaves.

---

[9] **allegations**—unproved charges; accusations.

[10] Jesuit—member of the Society of Jesus, a Roman Catholic religious order for men founded by Ignatius of Loyola in 1534.

[11] **travesty**—absurd imitation [of justice].

During 1741 and 1742, some 160 slaves were accused of conspiring against the city of New York. Only seventeen were acquitted. . . .

The Slave Revolts
by William Loren Katz

The greatest fear of the slaveholder was not the escape of his slaves but possible revolts. A Carolina planter warned a friend: "The love of freedom, sir, is an inborn sentiment. . . . It springs forth and flourishes with a vigor that defies all check. There never have been slaves in any country, who have not seized the first favorable opportunity to revolt." It was not surprising, then, when a visitor to the South reported that "I have known times here when not a single planter had a calm night's rest. They never lie down to sleep without . . . loaded pistols at their sides."

Slave revolts were planned, or took place, in Southern cities, on plantations, or aboard ships. Except for those at sea, none could succeed, for the entire armed might of the local and state militia and the armed forces of the federal government stood ready to crush any rebellion. But plots and revolts marked the entire history of Negro slavery in the United States. They were a last, hopeless, and desperate battle against a system that held lives in contempt and destroyed human dignity.

Prosser's Plot
In 1800, Gabriel Prosser, a Virginia slave, prepared thousands of his fellow bondsmen to attack Richmond. A violent storm saved the city. It washed out bridges and flooded roads and before Gabriel could regroup his men, the plot was betrayed by two house slaves. The leaders were arrested, tried, and sentenced to death. One told the court that he had only done for his people what George Washington had done for America: "I have ventured my life . . . to obtain the liberty of my countrymen."

The Denmark Vesey Plot

In Charleston, South Carolina in 1822, a vast slave plot was uncovered. Its leader was a tall, muscular carpenter, Denmark Vesey, who spoke several languages. As a young man, Vesey had bought his own liberty when he won a $1,500 raffle. The conspiracy had been planned for four years, and the slaves involved had hidden away weapons and ammunition. The authorities, given information by two house slaves, arrested 131 suspects. An attempt to rescue the slaves was feared. Federal troops stood by to protect the city as the leaders were led to the gallows. Before the traps were sprung the doomed men called on slaves everywhere to revolt until freedom was theirs.

The Nat Turner Rebellion

It was the Nat Turner revolt of 1831 which so frightened the South that at least one state considered giving up slavery. Turner led his small band of Virginia slaves from plantation to plantation, murdering slaveholding families and recruiting their slaves. Before the rebellion was finally smashed, federal troops, artillery, and state forces had to be called in. For two months a panic-stricken Virginia legislature talked seriously of ending Negro slavery. But the lawmakers decided, instead, to crush all slave resistance with more severe laws and tighter controls over slaves. Since Nat Turner was a preacher and an educated man, Southern states increased their control of black preachers and the education of slaves. "To see you with a book in your hand, they would almost cut your throat," recalled one slave.

A member of the Virginia legislature admitted how far they would go to keep slaves from learning.

> We have, as far as possible, closed every avenue by which light might enter their minds. If you could extinguish the capacity to see the

light, our work would be completed; they would then be on a level with the beasts of the field, and we should be safe! . . .

The spirit of defiance among slaves did not end with the death of Nat Turner. Two mutinies aboard the ships of the slave trade were successful.

Mutiny on the Amistad

In 1839, Cinque, son of an African king, led slaves in a revolt aboard the *Amistad*. "I would not see you serve to white men," he told them. "You had better be killed than live many moons in misery. . . . I could die happy if by dying I could save so many of my brothers from the bondage of the white men." Cinque and his men seized the ship and tried to sail it back to Africa. By the treachery of the slave dealers, whose lives they had spared, they were landed on the Connecticut coast and captured. Cinque and the others were finally freed by the Supreme Court of the United States after a lengthy battle led by ex-President John Quincy Adams, who served as their lawyer.

Mutiny on the Creole

In 1841, a slave named Madison Washington led a revolt aboard the *Creole* that also succeeded. Washington rescued his own lovely wife, who was held below decks with other slave women. The lives of the white members of the crew had been spared on promises of good behavior. However, the crew proved to be treacherous and the slaves wanted to execute them. At this point, Washington said: "We have got our liberty, and that is all that we have been fighting for. Let no more blood be shed." The free men and women of the *Creole* sailed to the West Indies where they lived out their lives in freedom.

Until Emancipation Day, slave men and women battled for their dignity and freedom in ways that appeared most practical. Many demonstrated the same raw bravery and stubborn courage as the Minutemen at Concord, or the ragged armies at Valley Forge.

QUESTIONS TO CONSIDER

1. Imagine you are on the jury at a trial of the slaves at Stono and in New York City. What evidence do you find in these accounts for or against the events having been the result of conspiracy?

2. In what ways were the trials in Judge Horsmanden's court like the Salem witch trials?

3. What do Prosser, Vesey, and Turner have in common? Is there any way their activities can be viewed as heroic? If so, how?

4. How is the behavior of both the mutineers and the crews on the *Amistad* and the *Creole* alike? How are they different?

Ka Le of the *Amistad* Writes John Quincy Adams

The Amistad *affair began when forty-nine members of the African Mendi people were captured and sold into slavery. They were shipped to Cuba, sold again, and put on board the* Amistad *for delivery to a Caribbean plantation. One captive, Cinque, freed himself from his chains, liberated the others, and led a shipboard revolt. The ship's cook and captain were killed in the struggle. When the Mendis' plan to sail back to Africa failed, the surviving crew members tricked them into sailing into U.S. waters. There they were taken into custody. Spanish colonial officials in Cuba sued for the return of the "property" and pressed charges for murder. American abolitionists worked for the Africans' release. The case ultimately reached the U.S. Supreme Court, which found in the Africans' favor. Former President John Quincy Adams, then serving in the House of Representatives, was on the Africans' legal defense team. While he was preparing his arguments, a defendant named Ka Le wrote him the following letter.*

Westville, Jan. 4, 1841

Dear Friend Mr. Adams:

I want to write a letter to you because you love Mendi people, and you talk to the grand court. We want to tell you one thing. Jose Ruiz say we born in Havana, he tell lie. We stay in Havana 10 days and 10 nights. We stay no more. We all born in Mendi—we no understand the Spanish language. Mendi people been in America 17 moons. We talk America language a little, not very good. We write every day; we write plenty letters. We read most all time. We read all Matthew, and Mark, and Luke, and John,[1] and plenty of little books. We love books very much. We want you to ask the Court what we have done wrong. What for Americans keep us in prison. Some people say Mendi people crazy, Mendi people **dolt**,[2] because we no talk America language. America people no talk Mendi language. American people crazy dolts? They tell bad things about Mendi people and we no understand. Some men say Mendi people very happy because they laugh and have plenty to eat. Mr. Pendleton come and Mendi people all look sorry because they think about Mendiland and friends we no see now. Mr. Pendleton say we feel anger and white men afraid of us. Then we no look sorry again. That's why we laugh. But Mendi people feel bad. O, we can't tell how bad. Some people say, Mendi people no have souls. Why we feel bad, we no have no souls?[3] We want to be free very much.

---

[1] Matthew, Mark, Luke, and John are books in the New Testament of the Christian Bible. Ka Le is saying he understands Christian beliefs. He is going to base his case on the principles that he knows Americans claim to believe.

[2] **dolt**—dull, stupid person.

[3] Ka Le says: Why would we feel so bad if we have no souls?

Dear friend Mr. Adams, you have children, you have friends, you love them, you feel very sorry if Mendi people come and take all to Africa. We feel bad for our friends, and our friends all feel bad for us. Americans not take us in ship. We were on shore and Americans tell us slave ship catch us. They say we make you free. If they make us free they tell truth, if they not make us free they tell lie. If America give us free we glad, if they no give us free we sorry—we sorry for Mendi people little, we sorry for America people great deal because God punish liars. We want you to tell court that Mendi people no want to go back to Havana, we no want to be killed. Dear friend, we want you to know how we feel. Mendi people *think, think, think.* Nobody know what he think; teacher he know, we tell him some. Mendi people have got souls. We think we *know* God punish us if we tell lie. We never tell lie; we speak truth. What for Mendi people afraid? Because they have got souls. Cook say he kill, he eat Mendi people—we afraid—we kill cook. Then captain kill one man with knife, and cut Mendi people plenty. We [would] never [have killed] captain if he no kill us. If court ask who brought Mendi people to America? We bring ourselves. Ceci hold the rudder. All we want is make us free, not send us to Havana. Send us home. Give us Missionary. We tell Mendi people Americans spoke truth. We give them good tidings. We tell them there is one God. You must worship him. Make us free and we will bless you and all Mendi people will bless you, Dear friend Mr. Adams.

Your friend,
Ka Le

QUESTIONS TO CONSIDER

1. From the text of the letter, what can you infer were the arguments made to return the Mendis to slavery?

2. What is Ka Le's position?

3. Which one of Ka Le's points seems to you to be most persuasive?

4. What defense do you think would be made for the people of the *Amistad* today?

Resistance

The Nat Turner Rebellion In 1831, Turner and several other slaves led an insurrection in Virginia, hoping that all black Americans would rise up and overthrow slavery. Many local whites, including Turner's owner and his family, were killed. At Turner's trial, a document supposed to be his confession was produced in court as evidence. Turner and nineteen others were hanged. White fear of rebellions became acute, and resulted in repression of slaves and support for the Fugitive Slave Laws. The drawing shows Turner's capture.

The *Amistad* Revolt Cinque, pictured here from a contemporary account, led a shipboard revolt on board the *Amistad,* which was carrying him and forty-eight other captured Mendis to a Cuban plantation. The ship's cook and captain were killed. Ultimately, the U.S. Supreme Court freed the Mendis. See page 115 for the full story. ▶

Deposite in the Clerks office for the
Southern District of New York August 31 1839

D.L. Recd 9th Novr. 1839.
No. 767.

JOSEPH CINQUEZ.

The brave Congolese Chief, who prefers death to Slavery, and who now lies in Jail in Irons at New Haven
Conn. awaiting his trial for daring for freedom.

SPEECH TO HIS COMRADE SLAVES AFTER MURDERING THE CAPTAIN &C. AND GETTING POSSESSION OF THE VESSEL
AND CARGO

"Brothers we have done that which we purposed, our hands are now clean for we have striven to regain the precious heritage we
received from our fathers. We have only to persevere, Where the Sun rises there is our home, our brethren, our fathers. Do not seek
to defeat my orders, if so I shall sacrifice any one who would endanger the rest, when at home we will kill the Old Man, the
young one shall be saved he is kind and gave you bread, we must not kill those who give us water.
Brothers, I am resolved that it is better to die than be a white man's slave, and I will not complain if by dying I save you.
Let us be careful what we eat that we may not be sick. The deed is done and I need say no more."

Mailed to Freedom Some people found novel ways to make their escape. Henry "Box" Brown had himself shipped from Richmond, Virginia, to Philadelphia, Pennsylvania. ▶

The Underground Railroad Escaping slaves often traveled by river after dark. From a wood engraving in *Harper's Weekly,* April 9, 1864.
▼

Bounty for Runaways Notices of runaway slaves gave detailed descriptions; any white citizen could take a suspected runaway into custody. There was a reward if the white citizen was right and no punishment if he or she was wrong or if the capture resulted in the suspect's injury or death.

"Paddyroller, Mean as Dogs" A slave patrol examines passes on a road south of New Orleans. Whenever slaves were off the plantation, they had to carry passes from their masters. The white men employed in the patrol were often cruel and arbitrary, beating slaves on the least excuse. From an 1862 wood engraving.
▼

◄ **Sojourner Truth** Freed by her New York owner in the 1820s, Truth became a vigorous opponent of slavery. Her voice was an influential one; she was received at the White House by Abraham Lincoln. During the Civil War, she raised money and supplies for the black volunteer Union regiments.

◄ **Harriet Tubman** The famous "conductor" on the Underground Railroad returned to the South nineteen times after her own escape to help her family and over three hundred other people reach freedom in the North.

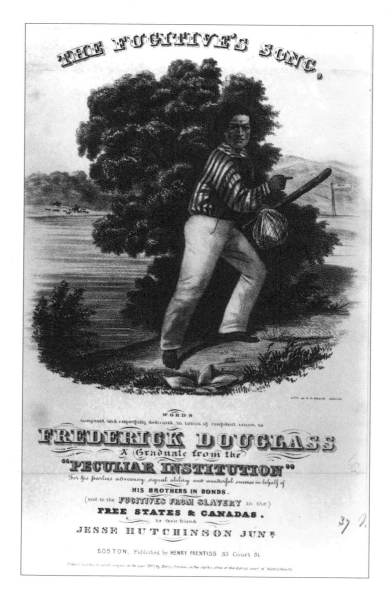

▲

Frederick Douglass Douglass, shown here in a book illustration, was an
agent and lecturer for the Massachusetts Anti-Slavery Society, publisher of the
antislavery weekly *North Star* (1847–64), advisor to President Lincoln, organizer
of two black regiments, marshal of the District of Columbia (1877–81),
and U.S. consul general to Haiti (1889–91).

Day-to-Day Resistance

BY PETER KOLCHIN

*Enslaved Americans found ways to resist other than armed revolt.
They could, for instance, make the management process as difficult
for whites as possible. Slaves regularly engaged in what historian Peter
Kolchin has called "silent sabotage." Work slowdowns, fake illnesses,
the mysterious disappearance of tools or supplies—all disrupted
the workings of a plantation. These activities probably were responsible for whites characterizing slaves as "lazy" and "thieving." But
such strategies allowed slaves to express their resentment and
anger without risking death or extreme physical punishment. They
also provided some secret pleasure for slaves who saw the increased
expenditures of time and effort their acts forced on slave owners.
More direct, however, was another course of action against daily
humiliation and injustice—confrontation. Historian Peter Kolchin
discusses this below.*

Like slave folklore, slave resistance can tell us much
about autonomy and communality in the antebellum
South. One of the most striking characteristics of that

resistance—aside from its very existence—is that it was largely the work of individuals. If collective forms of resistance such as rebellion and **marronage**[1] were minor features of Southern society, the types of resistance that *were* widespread featured slaves who acted alone or in very small groups rather than as **communal**[2] representatives. Slaves learned by experience that such individual resistance—although by no means risk-free—had the greatest chance of success.

This was true of both confrontations and flight. Physical confrontation initiated by a large group of slaves was indistinguishable from revolt in the eyes of most slave owners, and invariably called forth swift and merciless response. Slaves who challenged a group of whites also faced almost certain repression, because the nature of the conflict transformed it from a struggle between two individuals into an **affront**[3] to the honor of those challenged; however they might respond in private, masters could not tolerate public assaults on their authority. Slaves who ran away found that they could travel most safely in a white-dominated world either alone or in pairs; larger groups of fugitives inevitably risked attracting attention and lost mobility. In short, the particular conditions under which Southern slaves lived permitted a significant degree of individual resistance but severely discouraged collective protest.

This should not be taken to imply an absence of cooperation among slaves resisting authority. Slaves joined together to **pilfer**[4] their masters' larders, as well as, less often, to burn their barns and poison their food.

---

[1] **marronage**—desertion, flight, or movement of people in response to repression.

[2] **communal**—collective; on behalf of the group.

[3] **affront**—insulting act; confrontation.

[4] **pilfer**—steal small quantities from.

Despite the existence of slave informers, many bonds-people[5] protected those accused of criminal behavior if that behavior was directed at whites rather than at other slaves, and slave owners trying to identify the perpetrators of vandalism or theft often ran into a wall of silence when they questioned their people. Fugitives rightly feared being betrayed by slaves seeking to **curry favor**[6] with authorities, but some runaways received food, shelter, and guidance from sympathetic blacks, both slave and free; Harriet Jacobs hid for seven years in the attic of her grandmother, a respected free black woman who kept her secret and eventually helped her escape to the North.

But although there was extensive cooperation among slaves resisting authority, this cooperation was almost always that of individuals. Slaves lacked any kind of institutional body like the Russian peasant commune, which represented a whole village or estate and made decisions on behalf of all peasants. Decisions to flee or confront authorities were not reached communally, through collective deliberation, but individually, through private deliberation; indeed, slaves planning to escape usually took care *not* to inform others and thus risk their chance at freedom. Although occasionally a large group of slaves, unexpectedly caught by a slave patrol in a forbidden night-time revelry, might put up spirited if **futile**[7] resistance, virtually never in the antebellum South did all the slaves on a plantation decide collectively to go on strike or run away, as serfs often did in Russia. The pattern of slave resistance in the antebellum South thus points to a complex environment that permitted extensive cooperation among slaves but at the same time severely limited the kinds of communal behavior that were possible.

---

[5] bondspeople—slaves.

[6] **curry favor**—win approval, gain favors.

[7] **futile**—hopeless, useless.

Examining when and why slaves resisted yields equally significant observations. The trigger for slave flight and confrontations almost always consisted of a violation by white authorities of commonly accepted standards of behavior. No matter how much they detested slavery, the balance of forces—and the need to get on with their lives, even under harsh conditions—prevented slaves from engaging in constant struggle against it; resistance was by no means random, or constant across time and space. Certain actions by slave owners and their agents, however, were clearly intolerable. These included most notably excessive or unjustified punishment—that is, punishment that exceeded "normal" **parameters**[8] or that was meted out for misdeeds not actually committed—but also a host of other breaches of civilized treatment, including separation of family members, sexual assaults, and arbitrary or erratic management. The death of an owner was also a particularly stressful time for slaves, because no one could be sure what would follow; estates were often broken up to pay off debts or satisfy claims of heirs, and at the very least the slaves would have to adjust to a new owner, who would want to establish his or her own authority and would be likely to have new ideas of how things should be done. It is not surprising, then, that such death occasioned heightened concern on the part of slaves, concern that could manifest itself in real (if **ambivalent**[9]) grief as well as flight and resistance to new rules and regulations.

Although there were variations in the circumstances surrounding decisions to run away or confront whites—confrontations and temporary flight were frequently impulsive acts, immediate responses to unacceptable behavior, whereas flight to the North more often came after considerable thought and even preparation—these

---

[8] **parameters**—standards, limits.

[9] **ambivalent**—of two minds, pulled emotionally in two directions.

decisions almost always rested on specific grievances that triggered the determination to act. In their autobiographies, fugitive slaves typically combined assertion of what Henry Bibb called "a longing desire to be free" with reference to some **catalyst**,[10] most often involving punishment, that caused them to act on that desire; Bibb decided to flee in 1835, when his Kentucky mistress began abusing him physically, "every day flogging me, boxing,[11] pulling my ears, and scolding." As this example suggests, abuse of a slave accustomed to relatively **lenient**[12] treatment was especially likely to provoke resistance. Frederick Douglass found hirer Covey's abuse especially hard to take because he had been used to the privileged life of a house servant in Baltimore; Isaac Throgmorton, sold to Louisiana after enjoying considerable freedom as a barber in Kentucky, found "all the privileges were taken from me" and decided to escape to the North. But virtually any substantial change was unsettling and therefore **conducive**[13] to resistance, both because it threatened established procedures and because it reminded slaves that those procedures were by no means **immutable**.[14]

In short, although a general hatred of slavery and yearning for freedom underlay slave resistance, particular circumstances provoked individual decisions to resist. Despite their bitter detestation of bondage, on a day-to-day level most slaves came to terms with their conditions—because they had little choice—striving all the while to maximize their autonomy and preserve as "rights" the little privileges they were allowed to enjoy. When those rights were violated, however, slaves were likely to respond. Their resistance thus points both to a

---

[10] **catalyst**—element causing a reaction.

[11] boxing—hitting.

[12] **lenient**—merciful.

[13] **conducive**—favorable.

[14] **immutable**—unchangeable.

shared if never precisely defined understanding of what was acceptable and what was unacceptable within the general framework of a hated system, and to a **conservative mentality**[15] under which slaves for the most part grudgingly made their peace with an oppressive reality but, when pushed too far, resisted behavior that violated that understanding.

If most slave resistance represented specific responses by individuals to **intolerable**[16] situations rather than revolutionary efforts to overthrow the system, the consequences were nevertheless often far-reaching. Unlike armed revolt, which invariably called forth severe repression, flight and confrontation produced highly variable—indeed, unpredictable—results. Slaves who struck whites or ran away too often could find themselves brutally whipped, sold down the river, or even killed, and most could expect to receive at least some physical punishment for their insolence. Many, however, were decidedly more fortunate. Some fugitives reached the North, and others remained on the loose for protracted periods in the South. Still others, together with slaves who confronted white authorities, gained **ameliorated**[17] treatment for themselves even under slavery. Every slave owner, overseer, and hirer had to consider, on a daily basis, how individual slaves would respond to specific treatment and whether a particular action—a whipping or a new rule—was worth the risk of the response it might provoke. Slaves who gained a reputation for standing up to authority often gained a measure of respect and tolerance from white authorities and secured for themselves greater freedom of action.

---

[15] **conservative mentality**—outlook that leans toward keeping things as they are, opposed to change, cautious.

[16] **intolerable**—unbearable.

[17] **ameliorated**—improved.

QUESTIONS TO CONSIDER

1. Why was slave resistance by individuals more common than resistance by larger groups?

2. Under what conditions did slaves most commonly strike back at their owners or run away?

3. What explanations does Kolchin provide for why slaves did not resist more often?

William Cornish: An Interview

Even some slaves who felt well-treated made the decision to seek freedom in the North and risk punishment if recaptured. William Cornish, interviewed in his home in Canada in 1863, had enjoyed privileges as a Maryland slave undreamed of by the average field hand. Well-liked by his master and trusted to travel freely, he was also a skilled craftsman and administrator who sought out employment as a farm manager. While his wages were paid to his owner, not to him, he was allowed to earn and save money of his own. It was not until the death of his owner that Cornish found out that his status as property overcame any respect he had earned in the community, despite his past relative freedom.

I was born on the Eastern shore of Maryland, and came here in 1856. I had a very good time down in Maryland, considering I was a slave. I didn't come here because I was abused; I came here just for freedom. That was my object. I was abused, too, in a manner, although I was never struck since I was a boy by anybody. Still, the others was. The masters were privileged to use them as they were a mind to. Still, I had a very good time. I prepared myself to run away from the time I was 17 years old until I did get away. I always had a hope that some day I should be free. I always had **sufficient**[1] confidence for that. I was raised almost as one of the children. The master told the whites there that he would treat me as he would one of his children. He never told me so, but I knew I was trusted with everything. I could go to Baltimore and stay a week or two, or go to a camp meeting. I would go and come back, so he had confidence in me, and didn't believe I wanted to leave him.

Well, he always promised us all our freedom. After he moved into town & quit farming, I hired my time,[2] and then I wouldn't go home only once in a while. I stopped with one man five years, and I hired every man on the farm. He had just the same confidence in me that my master had, and wouldn't **suffer**[3] any **hand**[4] to come on the farm only what I hired. He paid my boss $55 a year for me, and I had all I earned over that. He used to carry on wood-chopping, and that I used to attend to for him—see to measuring it, and see what hauls he had in the bush, just as I did for my old boss. My master told me I might pay my wages to his son, who kept store in town, and go about like a freeman. But I hated to leave this man Jones, because I loved him like a brother. Then I worked for a man by the name of Skinner, and got some money. He said he couldn't get along without me, any way. I leaves there and goes up in Caroline county. The old man had five sons, three older than I am, and two younger. There were about thirty of us slaves. When the old man died, I was 25 miles from him, working for a Methodist preacher. The Dr. comes up to me and says, "William

---

[1] **sufficient**—enough.

[2] **hired my time**—worked for wages.

[3] **suffer**—allow, permit.

[4] **hand**—hired laborer.

Cornish, your master's dead." Said I, "Has he left a will?" Said he, "No." Said I, "Well, all is, we are all slaves." "No," said he, "you may be recorded **manumitted**."[5] "No," said I, "he who isn't true to God won't be true to man." I was much grieved. My heart ached. I thought it was a thing impossible for me ever to serve anybody else. Nobody knows what feelings I had. I waited about a month from that time, and then I went down to see the boys[6] at Cambridge, which was my family home. I see the young man, Thomas J. Dale, and I says to him these words, "Young Master Thomas, old master is dead, and I want my freedom." I said, "The last door to freedom is now shut," and I told him, "It is a thing impossible for me now to outlive all his children and grandchildren." "Well," says he, "William, it is bad." Then I goes to a lawyer, Mr. Josiah Bailey, that I used to go to school to sometimes, and I said, "Mr. Bailey, my old master is dead, and I want my freedom. I don't want run away freedom, but still," I says, "I want to be free." He says to me, "William Cornish, if you want to buy yourself, it is a thing you can't do now, because you are not divided;[7] you belong to the estate." I says, "Mr. Bailey, can't I go & petition, or can't his Executors petition, the Orphan Court[8] to have me **appraised**,[9] and with that appraisement give me the privilege of buying myself?" He says, "William Cornish, you've got more sense than me. You can do that. I never thought of that." I went to the Executors & they consented to that, and each one of the sons signed his name to the paper. I was appraised at $400. Thomas Dale said if I thought it was too much, each one would give me five dollars apiece. After I had

---

[5] **manumitted**—legally freed.

[6] the boys—his owner's sons.

[7] you are not divided—not specially singled out in the will.

[8] Orphan Court—court that ruled on matters related to the outcome of a dead person's possessions and children.

[9] **appraised**—evaluated, priced.

made two payments, one of $45 & the other of $60, I took my papers and showed them to a man, and he said they were not good for anything—that nothing was said about what was to be done with me after I had paid the money, and that if I paid 399 dollars and 99 cents, the heirs could sell me if they pleased. So that woke me up. I went to Mr. Wingate, who was one of the Judges of the Court, and told him I wasn't satisfied with my papers. He says, "Them boys wouldn't rob you of your freedom for anything in the world." Still I didn't feel satisfied, and I went home. I had about $200 worth of property, and I left in Sheriff Douglass's hand $75 in cash, and property that would sell for $100 more, I suppose, to be turned into cash and paid to these heirs. In the Summer of 1856 my mother came to my place and said, "The estate is going to take you in again." I said, "But I won't serve them." "Oh, what are you going to do?" said she. I found the old woman was pretty suspicious, so I thought I wouldn't say anything more to her. I had tried my wife before, but she didn't like the idea of my running away and leaving her folks, and burst out crying, so I never said anything more to her. I goes up to a camp-meeting in Caroline County and sees my young boss. I was carrying some water to a tent and he came along and said, "William, I want to see you in a day or two." I thought about what my mother had told me, and said, "You can see me now." He says to me, "William, Josiah (that was one of his brothers) is dead, and his estate is over $4000 in debt, and it will take all his personal property to pay it." I said, "That money is called for immediately?" "No, William," said he, "I am going to petition the Orphan Court to have a private sale." I said, "That is hard." "Yes," said he, "William, it is hard." And I believe the fellow felt sorry himself. "Well," said I, "I will attend to it about Saturday." He said, "Any time will do in the course of two or three weeks." When I told him that, I was sincere, and meant to do it. I thought I would go to some friend, who knew more about such things than I did, and ask him about it; so I went to an old Quaker and told him my circumstances, and he said, "If I was in your place, I would run away." My wife and mother were at the camp-meeting, and I went to them and said that I was going to Vienna, twenty miles off, to work; and I told them not to be noways uneasy if I shouldn't be at home. I left the camp on Saturday, and Saturday night I was up in the State of Delaware. I had no trouble in getting here at all. A man took me in a wagon and carried me about 30 miles on Sunday night; another man took me in the daytime on Monday, about 12 o'clock, and he traveled with me until about a half hour of the sun,[10] with a fast horse. He told me to go to another man, and I had to walk about two miles & a half & stayed there all Monday night and all day Tuesday. That night, he traveled with me about four or five miles on foot. He placed me in the hands of another man, who took me in a wagon and carried me about thirty miles that night, and then I got out and walked into Wilmington. There I took the cars,[11] Wednesday, for Philadelphia. Eleven days from the time I started, I was in Canada.

I have had very bad luck since I have been here. I was sick for six or eight months after I got here. My wife came out three months after. She was taken sick, and there were three weeks that I couldn't go out, but had to stay there and just turn her over in bed. I have buried three children since I have been here, and have had six children in all. The poorest day I ever see out here, I would rather be here than be with the best slaveholder that lives in the South, and I have seen slaves out there that were better treated than they can treat themselves here. I feel for the United States, even now, long as I have been [here]. I have got some good friends . . . but even

---

[10] a half hour of the sun—30 minutes before sundown.
[11] the cars—railroad cars.

now, if I see a Southerner come here, I cannot treat him with scorn, as some do, such are my feelings for the country because there are as good people in the South as there are anywhere, and so there in the North; and there are men in the South just as bitterly opposed to slavery as any in the North or here.

QUESTIONS TO CONSIDER

1. Why do you think Cornish's owner permitted him so many privileges? Why might such practices be in a slave owner's interest?

2. What did Cornish realize about the papers his master's executors gave him?

3. Cornish says he had always meant to try to escape from slavery. Why do you think he waited so long?

Slave Life and Culture

African-American Language

BY NATHAN IRVIN HUGGINS

Slavery completely uprooted individuals and took them against their will away from the lives they had known. The first Africans who came to America had much of their original culture destroyed. Most remarkable is that they and their descendants were able to preserve any of their African ways. Not only did they do so, but they created a distinctive, new, African-American culture. Language is a major aspect of culture, and, by studying a people's language, scholars can learn much about a people's values and customs. Here the historian Nathan Irvin Huggins describes how the language of slaves in America developed.

Communication was also necessary as a tool of trade. European traders and their African partners had to find words and signs—a code—which would allow their business with one another to advance with minimal misunderstanding. So language on both sides— African and European—reduced itself to bare simplicity, free of subtleties and complexities. There developed languages of European and African vocabulary and simplified **syntax**.[1] Such blends, based on African with Portuguese, French, and English, became the *linguae francae*[2] of the Atlantic basin.

The **pidgin**[3] languages that served the traders also allowed the captives to understand and be understood. The slave traders, and later the slave owners, preferred to mix the Africans, avoiding concentrating any one people together. This strategy rested on the desire to play on traditional hostilities and language differences so as to prevent conspiracies and uprisings. Yet, this mixture of tongues itself encouraged the invention of new languages. African languages within language families were not so dissimilar that those who would put forth effort could not be understood. Out of the mix and flux of peoples, various pidgins were born.

Children, despite the shock of rupture, found it easy to mouth new sounds for old meanings. Adults, on the other hand, would know how a thing was supposed to be said, and they would never feel new words approximated what they meant to say. They would always be uneasy that they were not being understood or that they had missed something said to them.

White men who wanted Africans to labor had to understand them and be understood. It might appear to the slave buyer, as he picked among newly arrived Africans, that they talked a "gibberish," and he might hope to have someone familiar with African languages to communicate for him. But his success as a master of African slaves would depend on his sharing a common language. He had to learn and contribute further to a workable pidgin dialect.

---

[1] **syntax**—the way in which words are put together to form sentences and phrases; the arrangement of words in sentences.

[2] *linguae francae*—French-Italian term for a hybrid language pieced together by people who speak different languages in order to do business.

[3] **pidgin**—hybrid, simplified mixture of two or more languages into one.

Circumstances and personality determined how the African fared. For some, the heart had been forever closed by tragedy, and the mind and spirit would never open to accept the new reality; the tongue would never untie itself in crude and alien sounds. Most, living among others like themselves, used the convenience of language to draw them together. There were a few whose company was mainly whites, whose language picked up more of the **cadences**[4] and sounds of Ireland or England. Others would find themselves among Indians, learning and teaching words. Occasionally, there would be one like Phyllis Wheatley, brought from Africa at the age of nine, petted in a New England household, educated on the standard Greek and Latin classics, who would write poetry in the language of Alexander Pope.[5] She was to be the second American woman, after Anne Bradstreet, to publish a book of poems in the English language.

Most African immigrants were to find their lives among others like themselves, with few whites about. Since they spoke most often to one another, there was little need to measure their words against an English spoken by whites. As generations passed and children native to America grew up, their language was to be an expansion and development of that used on the plantations. It would be their native tongue—thought in and spoken in as a natural thing—not artificial and strained as it had been with their mothers and fathers. It was familiar to them, just as it would have become familiar to whites with whom they spoke. Thus, their masters, now also a native American generation, could describe them as "country born" and speaking a "good" or "sensibile" English, even though it was no less the language of black men and women on plantations.

---

[4] **cadences**—rhythmic flow and rising and falling tones of a spoken language.

[5] Alexander Pope—famous eighteenth-century English poet.

English settlers made little effort to teach Africans English and made none to learn African languages; but each people had to find a halfway point. As they both became more skillful at it, the whites would come to consider the blacks more "sensible."

White men and women also became more "sensible" as time went on. Their tongues became accustomed to "goober," "tote," "gumbo," "banjo," "cooter," "chigger," "yam," "okra," "juke," and other such words from Africa. They picked up word patterns and tonalities as well. Through the generations following the first "country born" of both races, black and white children grew up together, playing the same games, using the same words. It would take a sensitive ear to distinguish native white from native black language. Many foreign visitors who came to the South in the nineteenth century remarked that English in the South had much to do with black influence.

Africa persisted in the language in subtle ways. Africans had often named their children according to the days of the week. There were day names for both boys and girls. Quashee or Quasheba, Cudjo or Juba, Cuba, Abba, Cuffee or Phibbi, all were to echo through two centuries, although sometimes in distorted form. English ears heard these sounds differently. So they were to be written in the plantation journals as Squash or Sheba, Joe, Abby, Cuff or Phoebe. White men might think that Juba was a dance and not Monday, that Cuba was an island and not Wednesday. They might think of the name Jack when they heard the name Quack. They might smile at what they heard as poor elocution, changing the name to sound right to their own ears. But black mothers and fathers continued to understand that the name stood for a given day or a season. In time, as Africa and England blended into America, black children would be given names like Monday, Friday, or Saturday, Winter or Summer.

Down into the nineteenth century, African names would survive. Ledgers of the slave merchant Dr. Louis de Saussure, dated 1864, list slaves named Rinah, Summer, Saturday, Kezia, Molsey, Sopha, Cinda, Tyra, Winter, Nelpey, and Sukey. Some were Anglicized versions of what had once been African; others were pure continuations of African names.

Language is a way of bringing peoples together, and it did bring diverse African words into the English-, French-, or Spanish-based Creoles.[6] But language is also a way of maintaining social distance among people, and it did that too in the new American tongues. Europeans and Africans had always made distinctions among themselves by how one used words. The higher orders marked themselves off from the lower by accent, tone, **diction**,[7] and vocabulary. So, too, in America, Negro speech and white speech became marks of social **disparity**.[8] Those blacks who mastered the white man's language were, in so doing, placing themselves socially at a remove from those blacks who did not. How a black person would come to speak American English would depend on more than opportunity, intelligence, and **facility**.[9] There needed to be a choice to **emulate**[10] white people, the ability to slip from one style of speech into another when the occasion warranted, and the willingness to bear the ridicule of fellow blacks who might think him a mimic and **sycophant**.[11]

White people, however, were anxious to keep their language to themselves. They wanted it as an emblem of the social superiority they felt to blacks and the lower

---

[6] Creoles—dialects of the original French and Spanish settlers of the Gulf Coast, especially Louisiana.

[7] **diction**—manner of expression, enunciation.

[8] **disparity**—lack of similarity.

[9] **facility**—ease.

[10] **emulate**—try successfully to equal.

[11] **sycophant**—person who fawns over and flatters important people in order to gain favor.

orders. They wanted to talk to one another, among blacks, and not have their meaning understood. They wanted language to serve in limited ways to communicate between themselves and slaves, but they also wanted it to remain **enigmatic**.[12] Language to them was a mark of civilization as well as a tool of communication, and they needed the sense of security a monopoly on good speech and literacy gave them. Furthermore, they knew that language transported ideas, and ideas could be weapons against established order. So, rather than finding a prideful, missionizing achievement in the **acculturation**[13] of Afro-Americans into English, the Anglo-Americans were protective and jealous. Above all, as far as it was possible, slaves were to be kept ignorant of the written word.

Blacks, too, had their secret codes, the most obvious and universal being drum sounds. Significantly, the earliest slave laws made the use of drums a criminal act for slaves. The need for secrecy would encourage blacks to hold on to African elements as long as they could. They also worked to speak in symbol, parable, and metaphor. They masked meaning by stories and song. White prohibitions against reading gave an almost **cabalistic**[14] weight to the written word (the Bible); there was something magical in translating marks on a page into meaning, in making the book "talk." Some learned to read as an underground thing, secret and forbidden.

Like all oppressed people, black Americans learned that in talking to whites, language could be a shield. Whites presumed that blacks knew little, and whites often showed the strain in trying to make themselves understood. It was easy enough to hide behind the barrier of language, to **feign**[15] ignorance or incomprehension.

---

[12] **enigmatic**—mysterious, puzzling.

[13] **acculturation**—adopting of traits or patterns of another's culture.

[14] **cabalistic**—referring to a small, secret group of people, plotters.

[15] **feign**—pretend.

To fall suddenly dumb before the white master's words was an instinctive evasion, a first line of defense.

An American language and style emerged out of the blendings of peoples—European, African, and Indian. Not merely did new words come into English, but cadences, rhythms, and inflections were affected. Characteristic ways the body moved in gesturing, the head was held, the eyes were cast, were formed from a relationship where two language codes were assumed, where one people was presumed **servile**[16] and **deferential**,[17] the other authoritative and masterful.

Aside from the human interaction, America itself called for invention, for expression beyond conventional language. The frontier wilderness, the rawness of the coupling of people and nature, the collisions of people with one another outside legal and social systems of control, the unspeakable grandeur of the country, all called forth a lexicon befitting the experience. When white men and black men exploded onto the frontiers or onto the riverboats and barges of the Ohio and Mississippi, they wanted to blow themselves up to the size of the country. The stories they told became incredible, challenging a reality that itself was beyond belief. And their words grew with strange inventions: absquatulate, slantendicular, cahoot, catawampus, spyficated, flabbergasted, tarnacious, bodacious, rampagious, concussence, supernatiousness, rumsquattle. Genteel Easterners would call such language gibberish and their inventors savages, but it was merely that America and Europe and Africa were building a language to fit the country.

---

[16] **servile**—submissive.

[17] **deferential**—respectful.

QUESTIONS TO CONSIDER

1. Why was it necessary for enslaved Africans to develop new languages?

2. Why is language an important indicator of what is happening in a culture?

3. How was language a "barrier" and a "shield" for slaves?

4. Which, if any, words that Huggins mentions are still current in America today?

Plantation Days

BY MARY ANDERSON

A treasure trove of memories from elderly African Americans who had been slaves was collected by the United States government during the Great Depression of the 1930s. At that time, interviewers from the Works Progress Administration (WPA) located people who had been born as slaves and recorded their recollections. These interviews provide a wealth of detail about what life was like under slavery, which had ended some seventy years before. The following first-person account comes from such an interview with Mrs. Mary Anderson when she was eighty-six years old.

I was born on a plantation near Franklinton, Wake County, North Carolina, May 10, 1851. I was a slave belonging to Sam Brodie, who owned the plantation. My missus' name was Evaline. My father was Alfred Brodie, and my mother was Bertha Brodie.

The plantation was very large, and there about two hundred acres of cleared land that was farmed each year. We had good food, plenty of warm, homemade clothes, and comfortable houses. The slave houses were called the quarters, and the house where Marster lived was called the great house. Our houses had two rooms each, and Marster's house had twelve rooms. Both the slave and the white folks' buildings were located in a large grove one mile square covered with oak and hickory nut trees. Marster's house was exactly one mile from the main Louisburg Road, and there was a wide avenue leading through the plantation and grove to Marster's house. The house fronted the avenue east, and in going down the avenue from the main road you traveled directly west.

Many of the things we used were made on the place. There was a **grist mill**,[1] **tannery**,[2] shoe shop, blacksmith shop, and looms for weaving cloth.

Marster had a large apple orchard in the Tar River low grounds, and up on higher ground and nearer the plantation house there was on one side of the road a large plum orchard, and on the other side was an orchard of peaches, cherries, quinces, and grapes. We picked the quinces in August and used them for preserving. Marster and Missus believed in giving the slaves plenty of fruit, especially the children.

A pond was located on the place, and in winter ice was gathered there for summer use and stored in an icehouse, which was built in the grove where the other buildings were. A large hole about ten feet deep was dug in the ground; the ice was put in that hole and covered. A large frame building was built over it. At the top of the earth, there was an entrance door and steps leading down to the bottom of the hole. Other things besides ice were stored there. There was a **still**[3] on the plantation, and barrels of brandy were stored in the icehouse —also pickles, preserves, and cider.

---

[1] **grist mill**—place for grinding grain into flour.

[2] **tannery**—place where animal hides and skins are made into leather.

[3] **still**—place for making whiskey.

There were about 162 slaves on the plantation, and every Sunday morning, all the children had to be bathed, dressed, and their hair combed, and carried down to Marster's for breakfast. It was a rule that all the little colored children eat at the great house every Sunday morning in order that Marster and Missus could watch them eat, so they could know which ones were sickly and have them doctored.

The slave children all carried a **mussel**[4] shell in their hands to eat with. The food was put on large trays and the children all gathered around and ate, dipping up their food with their mussel shells, which they used for spoons. Those who refused to eat or those who were ailing in any way had to come back to the great house for their meals and medicine until they were well. Sunday was a great day on the plantation. Everybody got biscuits Sundays. The slave women went down to Marster's for their Sunday allowance of flour.

Marster had three children, one boy named Dallas, and two girls, Bettie and Carrie. He would not allow slave children to call his children "Marster" and "Missus" unless the slave said "Little Marster" or "Little Missus." Marster's children and the slave children played together. I went around with the baby girl, Carrie, to other plantations visiting. She taught me how to talk low[5] and how to act in company. My association with white folks and my training while I was a slave is why I talk like white folks.

We were allowed to have prayer meetings in our homes, and we also went to the white folks' church. They would not teach any of us to read and write. Books and papers were forbidden.

---

[4] **mussel**—shellfish like a clam or oyster.

[5] low—softly.

QUESTIONS TO CONSIDER

1. What evidence do you find that the plantation owners were concerned about the health of the slave children?

2. What reasons might slave owners have had for being so concerned about the health of their slaves?

3. What kind of picture of slave life does Mary Anderson paint in this interview?

Slave Marriages

BY HERBERT G. GUTMAN

Using data gathered from plantation records, birth and death records, letters, and diaries, scholars have been able to put together a highly detailed picture of slave life. In the following excerpt from his book, The Black Family in Slavery and Freedom, 1750–1925, *historian Herbert G. Gutman looks at the records from a single plantation, Good Hope, in South Carolina. These documents are of particular interest because Good Hope's owner was an absentee landlord. He directed the operations there from a distance and did little to interfere directly with the domestic lives of his slaves. He kept detailed, careful records about his slaves' births, deaths, and marriages. Gutman's analysis of these records shows how slaves preserved family life. The stability and long duration of slave marriages and the evidence of extensive kin systems at Good Hope are proof that enslaved Americans were determined to resist the destructive effects of slavery on families.*

Most plantation [records] rarely listed a father's name . . . because a slave child's status followed that of its mother. The father's name did not have to be recorded. Because it listed most fathers' names, and also because of its relative completeness and the length of time it covered, the Good Hope birth register is an unusual historical document. The first recorded birth occurred in Africa in 1760 and the last ninety-seven years later, three years before Abraham Lincoln's election to the presidency. Listing the names of at least six blacks born in eighteenth-century Africa and twelve others not yet ten years old when the Civil War started, the birth register included more than two hundred slave men, women, and children and covered nearly the entire formative Afro-American experience: birth in Africa, enslavement, South Carolina plantation slavery, the development of an adaptive slave culture, emancipation, and finally life as legally free men and women.

In 1857, when the last recorded slave birth occurred, 175 men, women, and children made up the Good Hope slave community and nearly all were linked together by blood and marital ties that reached back into the eighteenth century. Children up to the age of ten were about one-third of the community, and about 10 percent of the slaves were men and women at least fifty years old. One hundred fifty-four children had been born between 1820 and 1857. About one in five died, mostly before their first birthday. None of the rest lived alone. Eleven had matured and married; the others lived either with one parent or, more commonly, with both parents. Twenty-eight immediate families made up this slave community. A widowed parent headed two families; three others contained childless couples; the rest each had in them a mother, a father, and their children. All but a few husbands and wives were close to each other in age. Eleven slaves, ten of them at least fifty years old, lived alone.

Kin networks linked slaves born in different generations, slaves listed as members of separate immediate families, and slaves living alone. A few examples illustrate the intensity of these ties:

In 1857, Patty, Captain, and Flora lived alone. Patty, born a mainland North American slave before her future owner's father Joseph Dulles left Ireland to become a Charleston merchant and an American slaveowner, was the oldest Good Hope slave and died in that year. Three generations of blood descendants survived her. An African by birth, the widower Captain was surrounded by married children and grand-children. In 1857, his oldest grandson, Charles, was twenty-one and his youngest, Zekiel, a year old. The widowed Flora lived in the same community as her married sons Dick and Mike, their wives, four grandchildren, six married half brothers and half sisters, and twenty nephews and nieces.

* * *

By 1857, Prince and Elsy, husband and wife for thirty years, had three married daughters (a fourth daughter had died in infancy), seven grandchildren, and twenty-nine nieces and nephews. Prince was Patty's son, and his younger married sister Clarinda and brother Primus lived in the community with their spouses and children.

* * *

Phoebe and Cuffee headed single-parent households. It had not always been so. Cuffee and Gadsey had been husband and wife for at least twenty-three years. She had apparently died. Cuffee did not remarry. In 1857, he lived with two grown sons; his other children had married, and at least ten grandchildren and a great-grandchild lived in the community. Probably widowed, Phoebe was still living with five of her nine children. Jack had been the father of the first four; Tom the father of the rest. Phoebe's oldest daughter was married and had the same given name as Phoebe's mother.

Two young and as yet unmarried mothers lived with their families of origin. The twenty-one-year-old Betty and her two-year-old daughter Leah lived with Betty's father, Burge, and his second wife, Rose. Betty had been named for her paternal grandmother. The seventeen-year-old Gadsey and her two-year-old daughter, Betsey, lived with Gadsey's mother, Duck, and her husband, Jake. Gadsey was not Jake's daughter; she had been born when Duck was living with Wilson.

Similar familial and kin connections existed among plantation slaves over the entire South in the 1840s and the 1850s. And the slaves living in the Good Hope community were typical in other ways of plantation blacks. The age at which a woman had a first child, the size of completed families, and the length of marriages in the Good Hope slave community hardly differed in other plantation communities.

Good Hope slave women bore a first child at an early age. The ages of twenty-three women whose first children were born between 1824 and 1856 are known: they had a first child at a median age of 19.6 years. The average age differed insignificantly. Three were not yet sixteen, and fourteen were between seventeen and twenty. Two each were aged twenty-one, twenty-two, and twenty-four.[1] . . .

Good Hope children grew up in large families. Among those born between 1800 and 1849, only one in seven had fewer than three siblings, and slightly more than

---

[1] The median age of fathers at the birth of a first child was older than that of mothers. The ages of nineteen out of twenty-four are known: their median age was twenty-three. Only two were under twenty, and one of them was fourteen.

half had seven or more siblings. Family size increased over time. Twenty-three women had a first child between 1820 and 1849, and not all had completed families by 1857. About four in five had at least four children; ten women had at least seven children.

* * *

Good Hope children also knew their parents well because most married couples lived in long-lasting unions. The ages of twenty-three of the twenty-six fathers living with their wives or their wives and children in 1857 are known. Among those aged twenty-five to thirty-four, the typical marriage in 1857 had lasted at least seven years, and for men aged thirty-five to forty-four at least thirteen years. July, for example, was thirty-eight years old in 1857, and he and Nancy had been married for at least sixteen years. Six of the nine men forty-five and older had lived with the same wife for at least twenty years. Sambo was not typical of these older men; born in 1811, he was not listed in the birth register as a father until his forty-fourth year, when he and Lena had a child. Lena's first husband, William, had died of fever in 1851 and left her with their infant son, William. The boy's paternal great-grandfather had been a slave named William. Sambo and Lena named their first-born daughter for Sambo's older sister Nancy. Unlike Sambo, other elderly men had nearly all lived in long marriages, lasting on the average at least twenty-four years. Gabriel and Abram each had lived with their wives at least thirty-four years.

QUESTIONS TO CONSIDER

1. What impression do you get about the slave community of Good Hope? Look over the bulleted paragraphs and list the topic of each. How would you describe the community?

2. What, in your opinion, does the author believe about slave marriages and their influence on the lives of slaves?

3. What conditions at Good Hope may have helped to preserve some African customs?

The Slave Life Cycle

BY ALLAN KULIKOFF

A slave's status as property dictated certain patterns in his or her life. Slavery shaped the ordinary business of living. Infancy, childhood, learning, courtship, marriage, family life, and old age —all had unique characteristics. In the following excerpt from Tobacco and Slaves: The Development of Southern Cultures in the Chesapeake, 1680–1800, *award-winning historian Allan Kulikoff examines the patterns of the slave's life, using data from plantation records in the Chesapeake Bay area of Virginia and Maryland before the Civil War.*

By the 1750s, a [distinctively] Afro-American life cycle had developed. Afro-Americans lived in a succession of different kinds of households. Children under ten years almost always lived with their mothers, and more than half on large plantations lived with both parents. Between ten and fourteen years of age, large numbers of children left their parents' homes. Some stayed with **siblings**[1] and their families, others were sold, and the rest lived with

---

[1] **siblings**—brothers and sisters.

other kin or unrelated people. Women married in their late teens, had children, and established households with their own children. More than two-fifths of the women on large plantations and a fifth on small farms lived with husbands as well as children. The same proportion of men as women lived in nuclear households,[2] but because children of separated spouses usually lived with their mothers, large numbers of men, even on big plantations, lived only with other men. . . .

Infancy

For the first few months of life, a newborn infant stayed [. . . with] his mother. A mother would take her new infant to the fields with her "and lay it uncovered on the ground . . . while she hoed her corn-row down and up. She would then [nurse] it a few minutes, and return to her labor, leaving the child in the same exposure." Eventually, the child left its mother's lap and explored the world of the hut and quarter. In the evenings, he ate with his family and learned to love his parents, siblings, and other kinfolk. During the day the young child lived in an age-segregated world. While parents, other adults, and older siblings worked, children were "left, during a great portion of the day, on the ground at the doors of their huts, to their own struggles and efforts." They played with age-mates or were left at home with other children and perhaps an aged grandparent. . . .

Beginning to Work in the Tobacco Fields

Black children began to work in the tobacco fields between seven and ten years of age. For the first time they joined fully in the daytime activities of adults. Those still living at home labored beside parents, brothers and sisters, cousins, uncles, aunts, and other kinfolk. (Even on smaller plantations, they worked with their

---

[2] nuclear households—households containing a father, mother, and their children.

mothers.) Most were trained to be field hands by white masters or overseers and by their parents. Though these young hands were forced to work for the master, they quickly learned from their kinfolk to work at the pace that black adults set and to practice the skills necessary to "put massa on."[3]

At about the same age, some privileged boys began to learn a craft from whites or (on the larger plantations) from their skilled kinfolk. Charles Carroll's plantations provide an example of how skills were passed from one generation of Afro-Africans to the next. Six of the eighteen artisans on his plantations under twenty-five years of age in 1773 probably learned their trade from fathers and another four from other kinfolk skilled in that occupation. For example, Joe, twenty-one, and Jack, nineteen, were both **coopers**[4] and both sons of Cooper Joe, sixty-three. Joe also learned to be a **wheelwright**[5] and, in turn, probably helped train his brothers-in-law, Elisha, eleven, and Dennis, nine, as wheelwrights.

Leaving Home

Beginning to work coincided with the departure of many children from their parents, siblings, and friends. The fact that about 54 percent of all slaves in single-slave households in Prince George's in 1776 were between seven and fifteen years of age suggests that children of those ages were typically forced to leave home. Young blacks were most frequently forced from large plantations to smaller farms. The parents' authority was eliminated, and the child left the only community he had known. Tension and unhappiness often resulted. For example, Hagar, age fourteen, ran away from her master in Baltimore in 1766. "She is supposed to be harbor'd in

---

[3] put massa on—satisfy their owners that they were working hard enough.

[4] **coopers**—barrelmakers.

[5] **wheelwright**—person who makes or repairs carriage and wagon wheels.

some Negro Quarter," he claimed, "as her Father and Mother Encourages her in Elopements, under a Pretense she is ill used[6] at home."

Courtship, Marriage, and Family Life

Courtship and marriage (defined here as a stable sexual union) led to substantial but differential changes for slave women and men. The process began earlier for women: men probably married in their middle to late twenties, women in their late teens. Men, who initiated the courtship, typically searched for wives by visiting a number of neighboring plantations and often found a wife near home, though not on the same quarter. Some evidence for this custom, suggestive but hardly conclusive, can be seen in the sex and age of runaway slaves. Only 9 percent of all southern Maryland runaways, 1745-1779, and 12 percent of all Virginia runaways, 1730-1787, were women. Few men (relative to the total population) ran away in their late teens, but numbers rose in the early twenties when the search for wives began and crested between twenty-five and thirty-four, when most men married and began families. Courtship on occasion ended in a marriage ceremony, sometimes performed by a clergyman, sometimes celebrated by the slaves themselves.

Slave men had to search their neighborhood to find a compatible spouse because even the largest quarter contained few eligible women. Some of the potential mates were sisters or cousins, groups blacks refused to marry. When they were excluded, few choices remained on the quarter, and youths looked elsewhere. . . . Most planters owned too few slaves, on too few quarters, to permit a wide choice of spouses within their plantations; furthermore, they could not afford to purchase the husband or wife. Inevitably, a majority of slave couples remained separated for much of their married life.

---

[6] ill used—badly treated; abused.

. . . After the relationship was consummated, the slave woman probably stayed with her family (parents and siblings) until a child was born, unless she could form a household with her new husband. Child-bearing, and the child rearing that followed . . . were highly important rites of passage for most slave women. Once she had a child, she moved from her mother's or parents' home to her own hut. The bonding between the slave mother and her child may have been far more important than her relationship with her husband, especially if he lived on another plantation. Motherhood, moreover, gave women a few valued privileges. Masters sometimes treated pregnant women and their newborn children with greater than usual solicitude. For example, Richard Corbin, a Virginia planter, insisted in 1759 that his steward be "Kind and Indulgent to pregnant women and not force them when with Child upon any service or hardship that will be injurious to them." Children were "to be well looked after."

Marriage and parenthood brought less change in the lives of most men. Many continued to live with other men. Able to visit his family only at night or on holidays, the nonresident husband could play only a small role in child rearing. If husband and wife lived together, however, they established a household. The resident father helped raise his children, taught them skills, and tried to protect them from the master. Landon Carter[7] reacted violently when Manuel tried to help his daughter. "Manuel's Sarah, who pretended to be sick a week ago, and because I found nothing ailed her and would not let her lie up[8] she run away above a week and was catched the night before last and locked up; but somebody broke open the door for her. It could be none but her father Manuel, and he I had whipped."

---

[7] Landon Carter was a plantation owner.

[8] lie up—stay in bed.

On large plantations, mothers could call upon a wide variety of kin to help them raise their children: husbands, siblings, cousins, uncles, or aunts might be living in nearby huts. . . .

Old Age

As Afro-Americans grew older, illness and lack of **stamina**[9] cut into their productivity, and their kinfolk or masters had to provide for them. On rare occasions, masters granted special privileges to favored slaves. Landon Carter permitted Jack Lubbar and his wife "to live quite retired only under my constant kindness" during the last three years of his life, and after over half a century of service. . . .

Many old slaves progressed through several stages of downward mobility.[10] Artisans and other skilled workers became common field hands. Although 10 percent of the men between forty and fifty-nine years of age were craftsmen in Prince George's, only 3 percent of men above sixty years of age held similar positions. Mulatto Ned, owned by Gabriel Parker of Calvert County, was a carpenter and cooper most of his life, but he had lost that job by 1750 when he was sixty-five. Abraham's status at Snowden's ironworks in Anne Arundel County changed from master **founder**[11] to laborer when he could not work full time. As slaves became feeble, some masters refused to maintain them adequately or sold them to unwary buyers. An act passed by the Maryland assembly in 1752 complained that "sundry Persons in this Province have set disabled and **superannuated**[12] Slaves free who have either perished through want or otherwise become a Burthen to others." The legislators uncovered a

---

[9] **stamina**—strength, resistance to illness or fatigue.

[10] downward mobility—increasingly lower social status and its accompanying standard of living.

[11] **founder**—metalworker.

[12] **superannuated**—elderly.

problem: in 1755, 20 percent of all the free Negroes in Maryland were "past labor or cripples," while only 2 percent of white men were in this category. To remedy the abuse, the assembly forbade **manumission**[13] of slaves by will and insisted that masters feed and clothe their old and ill slaves. If slaveholders failed to comply, they could be fined four pounds for each offense. . . .

Since husbands and wives, fathers and children, and friends and kinfolk were often physically separated, they had to devise ways of maintaining their close ties. At night and on Sundays and holidays, fathers and other kinfolk visited those family members who lived on other plantations. Fathers on occasion had regular visiting rights. Landon Carter's Guy, for instance, visited his wife (who lived on another quarter) every Monday evening. These visits symbolized the solidarity of slave families and permitted kinfolk to renew their friendships but did not allow nonresident fathers to participate in the daily rearing of their children.

Even though this forced separation of husbands from wives and children from parents tore slave families apart, slaves managed to create kinship networks from this destruction. Slave society was characterized by hundreds of connected and interlocking kinship networks that stretched across many plantations. A slave who wanted to run away would find kinfolk, friends of kinfolk, or kinfolk of friends along his route willing to harbor him for a while. As kinship networks among Afro-American slaves grew ever larger, the proportion of runaways who were harbored for significant periods of time on slave quarters seems to have increased in both Maryland and Virginia.

There were three different reasons for slaves to use this underground. [*The first reason*] Some blacks, like

---

[13] **manumission**—freeing.

Harry—who left his master in 1779, stayed in the neighborhood for a few weeks, and then took off for Philadelphia—used their friends' and kinfolk's hospitality to reach freedom. [*The second reason*] Others wanted to visit. About 27 percent of all runaways from southern Maryland mentioned in newspaper advertisements from 1745 to 1779 (and 54 percent of all those whose destinations were described by masters) ran away to visit. For example, Page traveled back and forth between Piscataway and South River in 1749, a distance of about forty miles, and was not caught. He must have received help from many quarters along his route. And in 1756, Kate, thirty years old, ran away from her master, who lived near Georgetown on the Potomac. She went to South River (about thirty miles distant), where she had formerly lived. Friends concealed her there. Her master feared that since "she had been a great Rambler, and is well known in *Calvert* and *Anne Arundel* Counties, besides other Parts of the Country," Kate would "indulge herself a little in visiting her old **acquaintance**,"[14] but spend most of [her] time with her husband at West River.

[*The third reason*] Indeed, 9 percent of the southern Maryland runaways left masters to join their spouses. Sue and her child Jem, eighteen months old, went from Allen's Freshes to Port Tobacco, Charles County, a distance of about ten miles, "to go and see her Husband." Sam, age thirty, lived about thirty miles from his wife in Bryantown, Charles County, when he visited her in 1755. Will had to go more than a hundred miles, from Charles to Frederick County, to visit his wife, because her master had taken her from Will's neighborhood to a distant quarter.

---

[14] **acquaintance**—friend.

QUESTIONS TO CONSIDER

1. How did kin relationships and networks help slaves to overcome some of the limitations of slavery itself?

2. Since young slaves were frequently sold away from their home plantations, and husbands separated from their wives and children, how did family relationships remain strong?

3. What does Kulikoff suggest is the reason such a large percentage of runaway slaves were male rather than female?

Family Life and Work

King Cotton Cotton was the crop of the South and its cultivation depended upon slave labor. Here a group of former slaves poses for a photograph in 1879.

Field Work Tobacco plantation workers cultivate the crop as shown in this wood engraving from *Harper's New Monthly Magazine*, 1856.

▼

Sitting in the middle of freshly picked cotton, these workers are preparing it for the gin, a machine that removed the seeds from the fiber. This photograph was taken by Timothy O'Sullivan on J. J. Smith's plantation in Beaufort, South Carolina, about 1862.

Former slaves working in the cotton fields in Alabama in the 1870s.
▼

Slaves on big plantations in the South lived in cabins like those pictured here, at the Hermitage plantation near Savannah, Georgia.

The interiors of the cabins were very simply furnished, and the family's domestic chores had to be done after work for the owner's family was completed. This May 14, 1864, pencil drawing by Edwin Forbes provides a view of women and children inside a cabin at Spotsylvania Court House, Virginia.

A Son's Pride

BY EMANUEL ELMORE

Not all slaves or slave owners lived on plantations. Emanuel Elmore worked at the Cherokee Iron Works in South Carolina. In these early factories, iron was smelted, refined, and formed into products that were sold by the owner. All of the workers at the Cherokee Iron Works were slaves. Elmore's skills won him great admiration from those around him, and his son, who was named for him, recalled his father's work with pride.

I was born on June 20th and I remember when the war broke out,[1] for I was about five years old. We lived in Spartanburg County not far from old Cherokee Ford.[2] My father was Emanuel Elmore, and he lived to be about 90 years old. . . .

---

[1] The Civil War began when Federal troops fired on Fort Sumter in April 1861.

[2] Cherokee Ford was the name of the place where the Cherokee River could be crossed.

I used to go and watch my father work. He was a **moulder**[3] in the Cherokee Iron Works, way back thare when everything was done by hand. He moulded everything from knives and forks to skillets and wash pots. If you could have seen pa's hammer, you would have seen something worth looking at. It was so big that it jarred the whole earth when it struck a lick. Of course it was a forge hammer, driven by water power. They called the hammer "Big Henry." The butt end was as big as an ordinary telephone pole.

The water wheel had fifteen or twenty spokes in it, but when it was running it looked like it was solid. I used to like to sit and watch that old wheel. The water ran over it and the more water came over, the more power the wheel gave out.

At the Iron Works they made everything by hand that was used in a hardware store, like nails, horse shoes and rims for all kinds of wheels, like wagon and buggy wheels. There were moulds for everything no matter how large or small the thing to be made was. Pa could almost pick up the right mould in the dark, he was so used to doing it. The patterns for the pots and kettles of different sizes were all in rows, each row being a different size. In my mind I can still see them.

Hot molten iron from the vats was dipped with spoons which were handled by two men. Both spoons had long handles, with a man at each handle. The spoons would hold from four to five gallons of hot iron that poured just like water does. As quick as the man poured the hot iron in the mould, another man came along behind them and closed the mould. The large moulds had doors and the small moulds had lids. They had small pans and small spoons for little things, like

---

[3] **moulder**—ironworker whose job was to form tools and other objects by pouring molten metal into molds.

nails, knives, and forks. When the mould had set until cold, the piece was prized[4] out.

Pa had a turn for making covered skillets and fire dogs.[5] He made them so pretty that white ladies would come and give an order for a "pair of dogs," and tell him how they wanted them to look. He would take his hammer and beat them to look just that way.

---

[4] prized—pried.

[5] fire dogs—a pair of metal supports for wood in a fireplace.

QUESTIONS TO CONSIDER

1. What advantages might a skilled slave such as Emanuel Elmore have had in his community?

2. How might these advantages have helped his friends and family?

3. How might they have affected his life after he was freed? How would his opportunities after emancipation differ from those of the slaves who had been field hands?

From Abolitionists
to Emancipation

Chapter 4

Petition of the People of Colour

BY SEVENTY-ONE "PEOPLE OF COLOUR, FREEMEN WITHIN THE CITY AND SUBURBS OF PHILADELPHIA"

In 1799, the Reverend Absalom Jones led a large group of free African Americans in petitioning Congress. They asked for protection from the oppression and violence that they and others "of like colour and National Descent are subjected." The petition focused on slavery, the international slave trade, and the kidnapping of African Americans, slave and free, that had increased as a result of the Fugitive Slave Bill of 1793. Reverend Jones submitted the petition to Representative Robert Waln, and he, in turn, introduced it in the House of Representatives on January 2, 1800. A huge debate ensued, and House members concluded that the petition had "a tendency to create disquiet and jealousy." They referred it to committee, where it was neglected.

To the President, Senate, and House of Representatives of the United States—

The Petition of the People of Colour,[1] Freemen within the City, and Suburbs of Philadelphia:

Humbly Sheweth,

That thankful to God our Creator and the Government under which we live, for the blessing and benefit extended to us in the enjoyment of our natural right to Liberty, and the protection of our Persons and property from the oppression and violence which so great a number of like color and National Descent are subjected; We feel ourselves bound from a sense of these blessings to continue our respective **allotments**[2] and to lead honest and peaceable lives, rendering due submission to the Laws, and exciting and encouraging each other thereto, agreeable to the uniform advice of our real friends of every **denomination**.[3] Yet while we feel impressed with grateful sensations for the Providential favours we ourselves enjoy, We cannot be insensible of the conditions of our afflicted Brethren, suffering under curious circumstances in different parts of these States; but deep in sympathizing with them. We are incited by a sense of Social duty and humbly conceive ourselves authorized to address and petition you in their behalf, believing them to be objects of representations in your public Councils, in common with ourselves and every other class of Citizens within the Jurisdiction of the United States, according to the declared design of the present Constitution formed by the General Convention and ratified in the different States, as set forth in the preamble thereto in the following words—viz—"We the People of the United States in order

---

[1] colour—color. This is the British spelling, which was used in the United States in the eighteenth century.

[2] **allotments**—shares.

[3] **denomination**—class.

to form a more perfect union, establish justice, insure domestick tranquility, provide for the Common Defence, and to secure the blessings of Liberty, to ourselves and posterity, do ordain &c."—We **apprehend**[4] this solemn Compact is violated by a trade carried on in **clandestine**[5] manner to the Coast of Guinea, and another equally wicked practised openly by Citizens of some of the Southern States upon the waters of Maryland and Delaware: Men sufficiently **callous**[6] as to qualify, for the brutal purpose, are employed in kidnapping those of our Brethren that are free, and purchasing others of such as claim a property in them; thus these poor helpless victims like droves of Cattle are seized, fettered, and carried into places provided for this most horrid traffic, Such as dark cellars and garrets, as is notorious at Northurst, Chestertown, Eastown, and **divers**[7] other places. After a sufficient number is obtained, then, are forced on board vessels, crouded under hatches, and without the least **commiseration**,[8] left to deplore the sad separation of the dearest ties in nature, husband from wife, and Parents from children thus pocket'd together they are transported to Georgia and other places and there inhumanely, exposed to sale: Can any Commerce, trade, or transaction, so detestably shock the feelings of Man, or degrade the dignity of his nature equal to this, and how increasingly is the evil aggravated when practiced in a Land, high in profession of the benign doctrines of our blessed Lord who taught his followers to do unto others as they would they should do unto them!—Your petitioners desire not to enlarge the volumes [that] might be filled with the sufferings of this grossly abused class of the human species (700,000 of whom

---

[4] **apprehend**—understand.

[5] **clandestine**—secret, especially for an illegal purpose.

[6] **callous**—hardened in feelings; unfeeling; insensitive.

[7] **divers**—diverse, meaning "several;" various.

[8] **commiseration**—expression of sympathy; compassion.

it is said are now in unconditional bondage in these United States) but, conscious of the **rectitude**[9] of our motives in a concern so affecting us, and so essentially interesting to [the] welfare of this Country, we cannot but address you as is Guardians of our Civil rights, and Patrons of equal and National Liberty, hoping you will view the subject in an impartial and unprejudiced light.— We do not wish for the immediate emancipation of all, knowing that the degraded state of many and the nature of their education would greatly disqualify for such a change; but humbly desire, you may exert every means in your power to undo the heavy burdens, and prepare way for the oppressed to go free, that every **yoke**[10] may be broken.

The Law not long since enacted by Congress called the Fugitive Bill, is, in its execution found to be attended, with circumstances peculiarly hard and distressing for many of our afflicted Brethren in order to avoid the barbarities wantonly exercised upon them, or through fear of being carried off by those Men-stealers, have been forced to seek refuge by flight; they are then hunted by armed Men, and under color of this law, cruelly treated, shot, or brought back in chains to those who have no just claim upon them.

In the Constitution and the Fugitive bill, no mention is made of Black people or Slaves[11]— therefore if the Bill of Rights, or the declaration of Congress are of any validity, we beseech that we as men, we may be admitted to partake of the Liberties and unalienable Rights therein held forth firmly believing that the extending of justice and equity to all Classes would be a means of drawing

---

[9] **rectitude**—uprightness of moral character.

[10] **yoke**—oppressive force.

[11] The petitioners are pointing out that an exception is not written into these documents for black people or slaves; thus, they argue, these were intended to be included.

down the blessing of Heaven upon this Land, for the Peace and Prosperity of which, and the real happiness of every member of the Community, we fervently pray.

QUESTIONS TO CONSIDER

1. What do you think moved these free men and women to petition Congress on behalf of the slaves?

2. Why didn't they request immediate emancipation? Give the reasons they cited. Might there be others?

3. What is the main argument given here for the petitioners' belief that Congress could remedy the situation?

from

Appeal

BY DAVID WALKER

One of the most radical of all anti-slavery documents was Appeal.
*Even the outspoken abolitionist William Lloyd Garrison found
its arguments too strong.* Appeal *was written in 1829 by a free
black man, David Walker, who wanted to instill pride in his
black readers and give hope that change would come someday.
In* Appeal, *Walker called for slaves to revolt against their masters.
He argued that "it is no more harm for you to kill a man who is
trying to kill you than it is for you to take a drink of water when
you are thirsty." Walker did not support the colonization movement which sought to help African Americans return to Africa. He
believed that America belonged to the people who had helped
build it. "America is more our country than it is the whites'—we
have enriched it with our blood and tears," he said. Within weeks
of its publication, copies of* Appeal *were discovered as far south as
Savannah, Georgia, and throughout the slave-holding states from
Virginia to Louisiana. By August of 1830, when Walker died,* Appeal
was in its third edition, the version from which these excerpts come.

My dearly beloved Brethren and Fellow Citizens.

Having traveled over a considerable portion of these United States, and having, in the course of my travels, taken the most accurate observations of things as they exist—the result of my observations has warranted the full and unshaken conviction, that we, (colored people of these United States), are the most degraded, wretched, and **abject**[1] set of beings that ever lived since the world began; and I pray God that none like us ever may live again until time shall be no more. They tell us of the Israelites in Egypt, the Helots in Sparta, and of the Roman Slaves, which last were made up from almost every nation under heaven, whose sufferings under those ancient and heathen nations, were, in comparison with ours, under this enlightened and Christian nation, no more than a **cypher**[2]—or, in other words, those heathen nations of antiquity, had but little more among them than the name and form of slavery; while wretchedness and endless miseries were reserved, apparently in a **phial**,[3] to be poured out upon, our fathers, ourselves and our children, by *Christian* Americans! . . .

. . . to my no ordinary astonishment, [a] Reverend gentleman got up and told us (colored people) that slaves must be obedient to their masters—must do their duty to their masters or be whipped—the whip was made for the backs of fools, &c. Here I pause for a moment, to give the world time to consider what was my surprise, to hear such preaching from a minister of my Master, whose very gospel is that of peace and not of blood and whips, as this pretended preacher tried to make us believe. What the American preachers can

---

[1] **abject**—utterly miserable; hopeless; humiliated.

[2] **cypher**—a symbol representing zero, usually spelled *cipher*.

[3] **phial**—vial, a small glass bottle.

think of us, I **aver**[4] this day before my God, I have never been able to define. They have newspapers and monthly periodicals, which they receive in continual succession, but on the pages of which, you will scarcely ever find a paragraph respecting slavery, which is ten thousand times more injurious to this country than all the other evils put together; and which will be the final overthrow of its government, unless something is very speedily done; for their cup is nearly full. Perhaps they will laugh at or make light of this; but I tell you Americans! that unless you speedily alter your course, *you* and your *Country are gone!!!!!*

. . . Let no man of us budge one step, and let slave-holders come to beat us from our country. America is more our country, than it is the whites'—we have enriched it with our *blood and tears*. The greatest riches in all America have arisen from our blood and tears:—and will they drive us from our property and homes, which we have earned with our *blood*? They must look sharp or this very thing will bring swift destruction upon them. The Americans have got so fat on our blood and groans, that they have almost forgotten the God of armies. But let them go on.

. . . I count my life not dear unto me, but I am ready to be offered at any moment, For what is the use of living, when in fact I am dead. But remember, Americans, that as miserable, wretched, degraded and abject as you have made us in the preceding, and in this generation, to support you and your families, that some of you, (whites) on the continent of America, will yet curse the day that you ever were born. You want slaves, and want us for your slaves!!! My color will yet root some of you out of the very face of the earth!!!!!! You may doubt it if you please. I know that thousands will doubt—they think they have us so well secured in wretchedness, to them and their children, that it is impossible for such things to occur.

---

[4] **aver**—declare positively; affirm; assert.

See your Declaration Americans!!! Do you understand your own language? Hear your languages, proclaimed to the world, July 4th, 1776—"We hold these truths to be self evident—that ALL MEN ARE CREATED EQUAL!! that they *are endowed by their Creator with certain unalienable rights*; that among these are life, *liberty*, and the pursuit of happiness!!" Compare your own language above, extracted from your Declaration of Independence, with your cruelties and murders inflicted by your cruel and unmerciful fathers and yourselves on our fathers and on us—men who have never given your fathers or you the least provocation!!!!!!

QUESTIONS TO CONSIDER

1. What in Walker's language might have made other abolitionists, such as William Lloyd Garrison, object to the message of the *Appeal*?

2. How does Walker compare the slavery of ancient civilizations to American slavery?

3. What does the popularity of the *Appeal* tell you? Who might have been reading it? How might they have come by a copy?

Speech at Pennsylvania Hall

BY ANGELINA GRIMKÉ WELD

Abolitionists were often very unpopular, even in the North. When Angelina Grimké Weld (1805–1879) delivered the following speech in Philadelphia in 1838, an angry mob raged outside the building. Their shouts frequently interrupted the speech, and the mob threatened to tear the hall down. Weld says their noise is proof that "slavery has done its deadliest work in the hearts of our citizens." Weld was a southern white woman who, with her sister, moved to the North to join the abolitionists. A devout Quaker with strong religious beliefs, she is also known for her activities as a feminist.

Men, brethren and fathers—mothers, daughters and sisters, what came ye out for to see? A reed shaken with the wind? Is it curiosity merely, or a deep sympathy with the perishing slave, that has brought this large audience together? [A yell from the mob without the building.] Those voices without ought to awaken and call out our warmest sympathies. **Deluded**[1] beings! "They know not what they do." They know not that they are undermining their own rights and their own happiness, **temporal**[2] and eternal. Do you ask, "what has the North to do with slavery?" Hear it—hear it. Those voices without tell us that the spirit of slavery is *here*, and has been roused to wrath by our abolition speeches and conventions: for surely liberty would not foam and tear herself with rage, because her friends are multiplied daily, and meetings are held in quick succession to set forth her virtues and extend her peaceful kingdom. This opposition shows that slavery has done its deadliest work in the hearts of our citizens. Do you ask, then, "what has the North to do?" I answer, cast out first the spirit of slavery from your own hearts, and then lend your aid to convert the South. Each one present has a work to do, be his or her situation what it may, however limited their means, or insignificant their supposed influence. The great men of this country will not do this work; the church will never do it. A desire to please the world, to keep the favor of all parties and of all conditions, makes them dumb on this and every other unpopular subject. They have become worldly-wise, and therefore God, in his wisdom, employs them not to carry on his plans of reformation and salvation. He hath chosen the foolish things of the world to confound the wise, and the weak to overcome the mighty.

As a Southerner I feel that it is my duty to stand up here to-night and bear testimony against slavery. I have seen it—I have seen it. I know it has horrors that can never be described. I was brought up under its wing: I witnessed for many years its demoralizing influences, and its destructiveness to human happiness. It is admitted by some that the slave is not happy under the *worst* forms of slavery. But I have *never* seen a happy slave.

---

[1] **Deluded**—misled; deceived.

[2] **temporal**—in life, as opposed to life after death; worldly.

I have seen him dance in his chains, it is true; but he was not happy. There is a wide difference between happiness and mirth. Man cannot enjoy the former while his manhood is destroyed, and that part of the being which is necessary to the making, and to the enjoyment of happiness, is completely blotted out. The slaves, however, may be, and sometimes are, mirthful. When hope is extinguished, they say, "let us eat and drink, for tomorrow we die." [Just then stones were thrown at the windows,—a great noise without, and commotion within.] What is a mob? What would the breaking of every window be? What would the leveling of this Hall be? Any evidence that we are wrong, or that slavery is a good and wholesome institution? What if the mob should now burst in upon us, break up our meeting and commit violence upon our persons—would this be anything compared with what the slaves endure? No, no: and we do not remember them "as bound with them," if we shrink in the time of peril, or feel unwilling to sacrifice ourselves, if need be, for their sake. [Great noise.] I thank the Lord that there is yet life left enough to feel the truth, even though it rages at it—that conscience is not so completely seared as to be unmoved by the truth of the living God.

Many persons go to the South for a season, and are hospitably entertained in the parlor and at the table of the slave-holder. They never enter the huts of the slaves; they know nothing of the dark side of the picture, and they return home with praises on their lips of the generous character of those with whom they had **tarried**.[3] Or if they have witnessed the cruelties of slavery, by remaining silent spectators they have naturally become callous—an insensibility has ensued which prepares them to apologize even for **barbarity**.[4] Nothing but the corrupting influence of slavery on the hearts of the

---

[3] **tarried**—stayed.

[4] **barbarity**—savage or merciless cruelty.

Northern people can induce them to apologize for it; and much will have been done for the destruction of Southern slavery when we have so reformed the North that no one here will be willing to risk his reputation by advocating or even excusing the holding of men as property. The South know it, and acknowledge that as fast as our principles prevail, the hold of the master must be relaxed. [Another outbreak of **mobocratic**[5] spirit, and some confusion in the house.]

How wonderfully constituted is the human mind! How it resists, as long as it can, all efforts made to reclaim from error! I feel that all this disturbance is but an evidence that our efforts are the best that could have been adopted, or else the friends of slavery would not care for what we say and do. The South knows what we do. I am thankful that they are reached by our efforts. Many times have I wept in the land of my birth, over the system of slavery. I knew of none who sympathized in my feelings—I was unaware that any efforts were made to deliver the oppressed—no voice in the wilderness was heard calling on the people to repent and do works meet[6] for repentance—and my heart sickened within me. Oh, how should I have rejoiced to know that such efforts as these were being made. I only wonder that I had such feelings. I wonder when I reflect under what influence I was brought up that my heart is not harder than the nether millstone.[7] But in the midst of temptation I was preserved, and my sympathy grew warmer, and my hatred of slavery more **inveterate**,[8] until at last I have exiled myself from my native land because I could no longer endure to hear the wailing of the slave. I fled to the land of Penn; for here, thought I, sympathy for the

---

[5] **mobocratic**—rule by the mob.

[6] meet—suitable; proper.

[7] nether millstone—lower millstone, the stone on which grain is ground into flour.

[8] **inveterate**—habitual; firmly established by habit or custom.

slave will surely be found. But I found it not. The people were kind and hospitable, but the slave had no place in their thoughts. Whenever questions were put to me as to his condition, I felt that they were dictated by an idle curiosity, rather than by that deep feeling which would lead to effort for his rescue. I therefore shut up my grief in my own heart. I remembered that I was a Carolinian, from a state which framed this **iniquity**[9] by law. I knew that throughout her territory was continual suffering, on the one part, and continual brutality and sin on the other. Every Southern breeze wafted to me the discordant tones of weeping and wailing, shrieks and groans, mingled with prayers and **blasphemous**[10] curses. I thought there was no hope; that the wicked would go on in his wickedness, until he had destroyed both himself and his country. My heart sunk within me at the **abominations**[11] in the midst of which I had been born and educated. What will it avail, cried I in bitterness of spirit, to expose to the gaze of strangers the horrors and pollutions of slavery, when there is no ear to hear nor heart to feel and pray for the slave. . . . But how different do I feel now! Animated with hope, nay, with an assurance of the triumph of liberty and good will to man, I will lift up my voice like a trumpet, and show this people their transgression, their sins of omission towards the slave, and what they can do towards affecting Southern mind, and overthrowing Southern oppression.

We may talk of occupying neutral ground, but on this subject, in its present attitude, there is no such thing as neutral ground. He that is not for us is against us, and he that gathereth not with us, scattereth abroad. If you are on what you suppose to be neutral ground, the South look upon you as on the side of the oppressor. And is

---

[9] **iniquity**—great injustice or wickedness; sin.
[10] **blasphemous**—contemptuous or irreverent about God or anything sacred.
[11] **abominations**—intensely disgusting or loathsome actions or practices.

there one who loves his country willing to give his influence, even indirectly, in favor of slavery—that curse of nations? God swept Egypt with the **besom**[12] of destruction, and punished Judea also with a sore punishment, because of slavery. And have we any reason to believe that he is less just now?—or that he will be more favorable to us than to his own "peculiar people"? [Shoutings, stones thrown against the windows, &c.]

There is nothing to be feared from those who would stop our mouths, but they themselves should fear and tremble. The current is even now setting fast against them. If the arm of the North had not caused the Bastille[13] of slavery to totter to its foundation, you would not hear those cries. A few years ago, and the South felt secure, and with a contemptuous sneer asked, "Who are the abolitionists? The abolitionists are nothing?"—Ay, in one sense they were nothing, and they are nothing still. But in this we rejoice, that "God has chosen things that are not to bring to nought things that are." [Mob again disturbed the meeting.]

We often hear the question asked, "What shall we do?" Here is an opportunity for doing something now. Every man and every woman present may do something by showing that we fear not a mob, and, in the midst of threatenings and revilings, by opening our mouths for the dumb and pleading the cause of those who are ready to perish.

To work as we should in this cause, we must know what Slavery is. Let me urge you then to buy the books which have been written on this subject and read them, and then lend them to your neighbors. Give your money no longer for things which **pander**[14] to pride and lust, but aid in scattering "the living coals of truth" upon the

---

[12] **besom**—broom.

[13] Bastille—a famous prison in Paris, France.

[14] **pander**—indulge the baser desires, feelings, or prejudices.

naked heart of this nation,—in circulating appeals to the sympathies of Christians in behalf of the outraged and suffering slave. But, it is said by some, our "books and papers do not speak the truth." Why, then, do they not contradict what we say? They cannot. Moreover the South has entreated, nay commanded us to be silent; and what greater evidence of the truth of our publications could be desired?

Women of Philadelphia! allow me as a Southern woman, with much attachment to the land of my birth, to entreat you to come up to this work. Especially let me urge you to petition. *Men* may settle this and other questions at the ballot-box, but you have no such right; it is only through petitions that you can reach the Legislature. It is therefore peculiarly *your* duty to petition. Do you say, "It does no good?" The South already turns pale at the number sent. They have read the reports of the proceedings of Congress, and there have seen that among other petitions were very many from the women of the North on the subject of slavery. This fact has called the attention of the South to the subject. How could we expect to have done more as yet? Men who hold the rod over slaves, rule in the councils of the nation: and they deny our right to petition and to remonstrate against abuses of our sex and of our kind. We have these rights, however, from our God. Only let us exercise them: and though often turned away unanswered, let us remember the influence of importunity upon the unjust judge, and act accordingly. The fact that the South looks with jealousy upon our measures shows that they are effectual. There is, therefore, no cause for doubting or despair, but rather for rejoicing.

It was remarked in England that women did much to abolish Slavery in her colonies. Nor are they now idle. Numerous petitions from them have recently been presented to the Queen, to abolish the apprenticeship with its cruelties nearly equal to those of the system whose place it supplies. One petition two miles and a quarter long has been presented. And do you think these labors will be in vain? Let the history of the past answer. When the women of these States send up to Congress such a petition, our legislators will arise as did those of England, and say, "When all the maids and matrons of the land are knocking at our doors we must legislate." Let the zeal and love, the faith and works of our English sisters quicken ours—that while the slaves continue to suffer, and when they shout deliverance, we may feel the satisfaction of *having done what we could.*

QUESTIONS TO CONSIDER

1. What are the reasons Weld gives for believing the church will not persuade the South to end slavery?

2. In what way is Weld affected by the angry mob outside?

3. What does Weld ask women to do to fight slavery?

4. In your opinion, what are Weld's most powerful arguments that action must be taken to end slavery?

from

The Fugitive Slave Act

As new states and territories were added to the United States in the 1830s and 1840s, the balance between slave and non-slave states was threatened. The Compromise of 1850 was a plan on which both sides could agree. It provided for the admission of California as a free state, the organization of New Mexico and Utah territories without restrictions on slavery, the adjustment of the Texas-New Mexico boundary, settlement of the Texas debt, and the abolition of the slave trade in the District of Columbia. Because Northern states had become lax in enforcing the Fugitive Slave Bill of 1793, a new Fugitive Slave Act was added. It was aimed directly at the Underground Railroad, which was helping approximately 1,000 slaves a year escape to freedom in the North. The new law was extremely harsh, encouraging the kidnapping of free blacks and denying a trial by jury to presumed fugitives. It paid the commissioners who enforced the law a $10 fee for each fugitive, free or slave, who was returned to slavery and only $5 if they freed him or her. The excesses that came about as a result of this act became fuel for the abolitionist movement and served as one cause of the Civil War.

An Act to amend, and supplementary to, the Act entitled "An Act respecting **Fugitives**[1] from Justice, and Persons escaping from the Service of their Masters," approved February twelfth, one thousand seven hundred and ninety-three.

Sections 1, 2, 3 are concerned with the formal provisions for appointing commissioners, who *"are hereby authorized and required to exercise and discharge all the powers and duties conferred by this act."*

Section 4 invests the appointed commissioners with *"authority to take and remove such fugitives from service or labor . . . to the State or Territory from which such persons may have escaped or fled."*

Section 5 specifies the penalties for failure to comply with **warrants**[2] issued under the provisions of the act:

Should any marshal or deputy marshal refuse to serve such warrant, or other process, when tendered, or to use all proper means diligently to execute the same, he shall, on conviction thereof, be fined in the sum of one thousand dollars.

Furthermore, should an arrested fugitive manage to escape from custody, the marshal or deputy would be liable to prosecution, and could be sued for *"the full value of the service or labor of said fugitive in the State, Territory or District whence he escaped."*

Commissioners were also empowered *"to summon and call to their aid the bystanders,"* and any failure to co-operate with such a summons would be a violation of the law:

All good citizens are hereby commanded to aid and assist in the prompt and efficient execution of this law, whenever their services may be required.

---

[1] **Fugitives**—people who have run away from danger, pursuit, or intolerable circumstances, such as slavery.

[2] **warrants**—written documents authorizing an officer to detain or seize a person or property.

Section 6

*And be it further enacted, That when a person held to service or labor in any State or Territory of the United States, has heretofore or shall hereafter escape into another State or Territory of the United States, the person or persons to whom such labor or service may be due . . . may pursue and reclaim such fugitive person, either by procuring a warrant from some one of the courts, judges or commissioners aforesaid, . . . or by seizing and arresting such fugitive, where the same can be done without process,[3] and by taking, or causing such person to be taken, forthwith[4] before such court, judge, or commissioner. . . ; and upon satisfactory proof being made, . . . to use such reasonable force and restraint as may be necessary, under the circumstances of the case, to take and remove such fugitive person back to the State or Territory whence he or she may have escaped as aforesaid.[5] In no trial or hearing under this act shall the testimony of such **alleged**[6] fugitive be admitted in evidence. . . .*

Section 7

And be it further enacted, That any person who shall knowingly and willingly obstruct, hinder, or prevent such claimant[7] . . . from arresting such a fugitive from service or labor, either with or without process as aforesaid, or shall rescue, or attempt to rescue, such fugitive from service or labor, from the custody of such claimant . . . ; or shall aid, abet, or assist such person . . . to escape from such claimant . . . ; or shall harbor or conceal such fugitive, so as to prevent the discovery and arrest of such person, after notice or knowledge of the fact that such person was a fugitive from service or labor as aforesaid, shall, for either of said offences, be subject to a fine not exceeding one thousand dollars, and imprisonment not

---

[3] process—having to get a legal document ordering the person to appear in court; the proceedings in a legal action.

[4] forthwith—right away.

[5] aforesaid—said before.

[6] **alleged**—presumed, supposed.

[7] claimant—the person who is claiming the alleged fugitive is a slave.

exceeding six months . . . ; and shall moreover forfeit[8] *and pay, by way of civil damages to the party injured by such illegal conduct, the sum of one thousand dollars for each fugitive so lost as aforesaid, to be recovered by action of debt . . . .*

Section 8 deals with the payments to be made to various officials for their part in the arrest, custody and delivery of a fugitive to his or her claimant. In effect, the financial incentives authorized under this clause turned the pursuit of escaped slaves into a species of bounty-hunting:

The marshals, their deputies, and the clerks of the said District and Territorial courts, shall be paid for their services . . . ; and in all cases where the proceedings are before a commissioner, he shall be entitled to a fee of ten dollars. . . . The person or persons authorized to execute the process . . . shall also be entitled to a fee of five dollars each for each person he or they may arrest and take before any such commissioner.

Section 9 stipulates that if the claimant suspects an attempt will be made to rescue the fugitive by force, then the arresting officer is required *"to retain such fugitive in his custody, and to remove him to the State whence he fled, and there to deliver him to said claimant."*

---

[8] forfeit—give up as a penalty.

QUESTIONS TO CONSIDER

1. In what way did the Fugitive Slave Act turn those people who pursued escaped slaves into bounty hunters?

2. How did the Fugitive Slave Act fit with the rights of individuals guaranteed by the Constitution?

3. How did the Act encourage the kidnapping of African Americans, including free ones?

The Fugitive Slave Act in the North

BY ERIC FONER

Columbia University history professor Eric Foner is an expert on the Civil War and has written many books and articles explaining its causes. In the following excerpt from an interview, he explains how the Fugitive Slave Act made slavery the business of the northern states, even though they had outlawed the institution.

The issue of fugitive slaves in a sense became one of the most powerful weapons in the hands of the Abolitionist Movement. The Constitution has a clause stating that fugitives from labor (slaves) must be sent back to the South if captured in the North. And this gave slavery what we call **extra-territoriality**.[1] That is, it made slavery a national institution. Even though the northern states could abolish slavery, as they did, they still could not avoid their Constitutional obligation to enforce the

---

[1] **extra-territoriality**—immunity from the power of local law; jurisdiction of a country's law outside its own territory. In other words, the laws of the South had to be observed in the North.

slave laws of the southern states. A fugitive slave carried with him the legal status of slavery, even into a territory which didn't have slavery.

Now, many of the states didn't do much about this. And that's why the Fugitive Slave Law of 1850 was enacted, which made the federal government responsible for tracking down and apprehending fugitive slaves in the North, and sending them back to the South. The Fugitive Slave Law of 1850, you might say, was the most powerful exercise of federal authority within the United States in the whole era before the Civil War.

And it's a very odd thing that a region, the South, which supposedly believed in states' rights and local **autonomy**,[2] pressed for this law which allowed the federal government to completely override the legal processes in the North: to send marshals in, to avoid the local courts, and to just seize people (they might be free born) and just drag them into the South as slaves. It shows that the South didn't believe in states' rights. It believed in slavery. States' rights was a defense of slavery. But when active federal power was needed to defend slavery, they were perfectly happy to utilize that also.

The Fugitive Slave Law had many features which seemed to violate the liberties of free white northerners. It allowed the federal government to deputize citizens, even against their will, and force them to take part in **posses**[3] or other groups to seize fugitive slaves. It also said that local courts could not **adjudicate**[4] whether a person was a slave or not. It was federal commissioners who would come in and hear testimony. And the slave was not allowed to testify. It was the testimony of the owner, or the person who claimed to be the owner, of

---

[2] **autonomy**—self-government.

[3] **posses**—groups of people empowered to assist in capturing criminals.

[4] **adjudicate**—decide in a legal case.

this alleged fugitive. And the commissioner would judge whether the owner's testimony was believable or not, and then send—as they usually did—the person back to slavery.

So the Fugitive Slave Law, was a very powerful instrument. It was utilized to gather up quite a few slaves, escaped slaves, or perhaps people who weren't slaves at all, who were free born, and send them back to the South.

Another thing is that it inspired quite a few thousand free Negroes in the North to flee to Canada. We usually think of the United States as an **asylum**[5] for liberty, of people fleeing oppression elsewhere in the world to come to the United States. It's a little jarring to remember that there were thousands of free born Americans who fled to Canada because their freedom could no longer be taken for granted within the United States.

Fugitive slaves had a tremendous impact on the development of the anti-slavery movement. First of all, a number of fugitives became very prominent abolitionist leaders and speakers. The most famous is Frederick Douglass, who escaped from Maryland. But there were quite a few others, [including] Henry Highland Garnet. They were living embodiments of the reality of slavery. When Douglass got up and talked about his life as a slave, it was hard to dismiss him as just a do-good-ing northern liberal who really didn't understand the situation in the South, as many southerners would claim. These are people who had experienced slavery firsthand.

But then the whole process, under the Fugitive Slave Law, of the federal government seizing people **galvanized**[6] opinion in the North in a way that the

---

[5] **asylum**—place of refuge, a safe place.
[6] **galvanized**—roused into action.

abstract question of slavery may not have done. You could think what you wanted about slavery hundreds of miles away, but when an individual comes to your community, a black individual fleeing marshals who are going to try to grab him and send him back to slavery, it puts slavery on a human level. It made people have to choose, am I going to abide by the law, or am I going to help this fellow human being who's in trouble? And many people who were not abolitionists at all felt they could not cooperate with the Fugitive Slave Law. And often it was violently resisted by people who were otherwise law-abiding citizens.

QUESTIONS TO CONSIDER

1. Why does Foner say that the South did not really believe in states' rights?

2. What, according to Foner, are at least three effects of the Act?

3. How did the Fugitive Slave Act ultimately work against the South?

4. What role does Foner say fugitive slaves played in helping to galvanize opinion in the North against slavery?

Dred Scott v. Sanford

THE U.S. SUPREME COURT DECISION

*The decision reached by the Supreme Court in the Dred Scott case
in 1857 is one of the most notorious rulings in the Court's history.
Chief Justice Roger B. Taney, who wrote the majority opinion,
declared that all blacks—slaves or free—were not and never could
become citizens of the United States. The decision also made the
1820 Missouri Compromise unconstitutional and permitted slavery
in all the country's territories. The case in which this appalling
decision was made was an appeal by a slave, Dred Scott. Scott's
owner had taken him into Illinois, a free state, and the territory
of Wisconsin, also free, before moving him back to the slave state
of Missouri. Scott argued that his residence in the free parts of
the nation undid his status as a slave. Taney, speaking for the Court
majority, decided against him. Abolitionists were furious and the
decision further divided the sides in the expanding national debate
over slavery.*

The plaintiff [Dred Scott] . . . was, with his wife and
children, held as slaves by the defendant [Sanford], in
the State of Missouri; and he brought this action in the
Circuit Court of the United States for [Missouri], to
assert the title of himself and his family to freedom.

The declaration is . . . that he and the defendant are citizens of different States; that . . . he is a citizen of Missouri, and the defendant a citizen of New York. . . .

The question is simply this: Can a negro, whose ancestors were imported into this country, and sold as slaves, become a member of the political community formed and brought into existence by the Constitution of the United States, and as such become entitled to all the rights, and privileges, and immunities, guaranteed by that instrument to the citizen? One of which rights is the privilege of suing in a court of the United States in the cases specified in the Constitution. . . .

The words "people of the United States" and "citizens" are synonymous terms, and mean the same thing. They both describe the political body who . . . form the **sovereignty**,[1] and who hold the power and conduct the Government through their representatives. . . . The question before us is, whether the class of persons described in the plea in abatement[2] [people of African ancestry] compose a portion of this people, and are constituent members of this sovereignty? We think they are not, and that they are not included, and were not intended to be included, under the word "citizens" in the Constitution, and can therefore claim none of the rights and privileges which that instrument provides for and secures to citizens of the United States. On the contrary, they were at that time considered as a subordinate and inferior class of beings, who had been **subjugated**[3] by the dominant race, and, whether emancipated or not, yet remained subject to their authority, and had no rights or privileges but such as those who held the power and the Government might choose to grant them. . . .

---

[1] **sovereignty**—supreme authority.

[2] plea in abatement—in law, an action to annul, or put a stop to, something, in this case Scott's status as a slave.

[3] **subjugated**—put under control.

The court think[s] . . . [Dred Scott] could not be a citizen of the State of Missouri, within the meaning of the Constitution of the United States, and, consequently, was not entitled to sue in its courts.

It is true, every person, and every class and description of persons, who were at the time of the adoption of the Constitution recognized as citizens in the several States, became also citizens of this new political body; but none other; it was formed by them, and for them and their **posterity**,[4] but for no one else. And the personal rights and privileges guaranteed to citizens of this new sovereignty were intended to embrace those only who were then members of the several State communities, or who should afterwards by birthright or otherwise become members, according to the provisions of the Constitution and the principles on which it was founded. . . .

It becomes necessary, therefore, to determine who were citizens of the several States when the Constitution was adopted. . . .

. . . [T]he legislation and histories of the times, and the language used in the Declaration of Independence, show, that neither the class of persons who had been imported as slaves, nor their descendants, whether they had become free or not, were then acknowledged as a part of the people, nor intended to be included in the general words used in that memorable instrument.

It is difficult at this day to realize the state of public opinion in relation to that unfortunate race, which prevailed in the civilized and enlightened portions of the world at the time of the Declaration of Independence, and when the Constitution of the United States was framed and adopted. . . .

They had for more than a century before been regarded as beings of an inferior order, and altogether

---

[4] **posterity**—descendants, those who would come after them.

unfit to associate with the white race, either in social or political relations; and so far inferior, that they had no rights which the white man was bound to respect; and that the negro might justly and lawfully be reduced to slavery. . . . He was bought and sold, and treated as an ordinary article of merchandise and traffic, whenever a profit could be made by it. This opinion was at that time fixed and universal in the civilized portion of the white race. It was regarded as an **axiom**[5] in morals as well as in politics, which no one thought of disputing, or supposed to be open to dispute; and men in every grade and position in society daily and habitually acted upon it in their private pursuits, as well as in matters of public concern, without doubting for a moment the correctness of this opinion.

And in no nation was this opinion more firmly fixed or more uniformly acted upon than by the English Government and English people. They not only seized them on the coast of Africa, and sold them or held them in slavery for their own use; but they took them as ordinary articles of merchandise to every country where they could make a profit on them, and were far more extensively engaged in this commerce than any other nation in the world.

The opinion thus entertained and acted upon in England was naturally impressed upon the colonies they founded on this side of the Atlantic. And, accordingly, a negro of the African race was regarded by them as an article of property, and held, and bought and sold as such, in every one of the thirteen colonies which united in the Declaration of Independence, and afterwards formed the Constitution of the United States. The slaves were more or less numerous in the different colonies, as slave labor was found more or less profitable. But no one

---

[5] **axiom**—self-evident or universally accepted truth.

seems to have doubted the correctness of the prevailing opinion of the time.

The legislation of the different colonies furnishes positive and indisputable proof of this fact. . . .

[T]hese laws . . . show, too plainly to be misunderstood, the degraded condition of this unhappy race. They were still in force when the Revolution began, and are a faithful index to the state of feeling towards the class of persons of whom they speak, and of the position they occupied throughout the thirteen colonies, in the eyes and thoughts of the men who framed the Declaration of Independence and established the State Constitutions and Governments. They show that a perpetual and impassable barrier was intended to be erected between the white race and the one which they had reduced to slavery, and governed as subjects with absolute and **despotic**[6] power, and which they then looked upon as so far below them in the scale of created beings, that intermarriages between white persons and negroes or mulattoes were regarded as unnatural and immoral, and punished as crimes, not only in the parties, but in the person who joined them in marriage. And no distinction in this respect was made between the free negro or mulatto and the slave, but this **stigma**,[7] of the deepest degradation, was fixed upon the whole race.

We refer to these historical facts for the purpose of showing the fixed opinions concerning that race, upon which the statesmen of that day spoke and acted . . . in order to determine whether the general terms used in the Constitution of the United States, as to the rights of man and the rights of the people, was intended to include them, or to give to them or their posterity the benefit of any of its provisions.

---

[6] **despotic**—like a cruel master, tyrannical; arbitrary.

[7] **stigma**—mark of shame, infamy, or disgrace.

The language of the Declaration of Independence is equally Conclusive:

We hold these truths to be self-evident: that all men are created equal; that they are endowed by their Creator with certain unalienable rights; that among them is life, liberty, and the pursuit of happiness; that to secure these rights, Governments are instituted, deriving their just powers from the consent of the governed.

The general words above quoted would seem to embrace the whole human family, and if they were used in a similar instrument at this day would be so understood. But it is too clear for dispute, that the enslaved African race were not intended to be included, and formed no part of the people who framed and adopted this declaration; for if the language, as understood in that day, would embrace them, the conduct of the distinguished men who framed the Declaration of Independence would have been utterly and **flagrantly**[8] inconsistent with the principles they asserted; and instead of the sympathy of mankind, to which they so confidently appealed, they would have deserved and received universal rebuke and **reprobation**.[9]

Yet the men who framed this declaration were great men—high in literary acquirements—high in their sense of honor, and incapable of asserting principles inconsistent with those on which they were acting. They perfectly understood the meaning of the language they used, and how it would be understood by others; and they knew that it would not in any part of the civilized world be supposed to embrace the negro race, which, by common consent, had been excluded from civilized Governments and the family of nations, and doomed to slavery. They spoke and acted according to the then established doctrines and principles, and in the ordinary language of

---

[8] **flagrantly**—glaringly, openly, badly.

[9] **reprobation**—condemnation.

the day, no one misunderstood them. The unhappy black race were separate from white by indelible marks, and laws long before established, and were never thought of or spoken of except as property, and when the claims of the owner or the profit of the trader were supposed to need protection.

This state of public opinion had undergone no change when the Constitution was adopted, as is equally evident from its provisions and language. . . .

[There] are two clauses in the Constitution which point directly and specifically to the negro race as a separate class of persons, and show clearly that they were not regarded as a portion of the people or citizens of the Government then formed.

One of these clauses reserves to each of the thirteen States the right to import slaves until the year 1808. . . . And by the other provision the States pledge themselves to each other to maintain the right of property of the master, by delivering up to him any slave who may have escaped from his service, and be found within their respective territories. . . . And these two provisions show, conclusively, that neither the description of persons therein referred to, nor their descendants, were embraced in any of the other provisions of the Constitution; for certainly these two clauses were not intended to confer on them or their posterity the blessings of liberty, or any of the personal rights so carefully provided for the citizen.

No one of that race had ever migrated to the United States voluntarily; all of them had been brought here as articles of merchandise. The number that had been emancipated at that time were but few in comparison with those held in slavery; and they were identified in the public mind with the race to which they belonged, and regarded as a part of the slave population rather than the free. It is obvious that they were not even in the minds of the framers of the Constitution when they were conferring special rights and privileges upon the citizens of a State in every other part of the Union. . . .

It would be impossible to enumerate . . . the various laws, marking the condition of this race, which were passed from time to time after the Revolution, and before and since the adoption of the Constitution of the United States. In addition to those already referred to, it is sufficient to say, that Chancellor Kent,[10] whose accuracy and research no one will question, states in . . . his Commentaries . . . that in no part of the country except Maine, did the African race, in point of fact, participate equally with the whites in the exercise of civil and political rights. . . .

To all this mass of proof we have still to add, that Congress has repeatedly legislated upon the same construction of the Constitution that we have given. . . .

The first of these acts is the naturalization law . . . [of] March 26, 1790, [which] confines the right of becoming citizens "to aliens being free white persons." . . .

Another of the early laws of which we have spoken, is the first militia law, which was passed in 1792, at the first session of the second Congress. The language of this law is equally plain and significant. . . . It directs that every "free able-bodied white male citizen" shall be enrolled in the militia. The word *white* is evidently used to exclude the African race, and the word *citizen* to exclude unnaturalized foreigners; the latter forming no part of the sovereignty, owing it no allegiance, and therefore under no obligation to defend it. The African race, however, born in the country, did owe allegiance to the Government, whether they were slave or free; but it is **repudiated**,[11] and rejected from the duties and obligations of citizenship in marked language.

---

[10] Chancellor Kent—a chief justice of the New York Supreme Court (1804–1814) and chancellor of New York (1814–1823). James Kent's written opinions and *Commentaries on the American Law* were accepted as a standard interpretation of the Constitution.

[11] **repudiated**—regarded as untrue.

The third act to which we have alluded is even still more decisive; it was passed as late as 1813, (2 Stat., 809) and it provides: "That from and after the termination of the war in which the United States are now engaged with Great Britain, it shall not be lawful to employ, on board of any public or private vessels of the United States, any person or persons except citizens of the United States, *or* persons of color, natives of the United States."

Here the line of distinction is drawn in express words. Persons of color, in the judgment of Congress, were not included in the word *citizens*, and they are described as another and different class of persons, and authorized to be employed, if born in the United States. . . .

No one, we presume, supposes that any change in public opinion or feeling, in relation to this unfortunate race, in the civilized nations of Europe or in this country, should induce the court to give to the words of the Constitution a more liberal construction in their favor than they were intended to bear when the instrument was framed and adopted. Such an argument would be altogether inadmissible in any **tribunal**[12] called on to interpret it. If any of its provisions are deemed unjust, there is a mode prescribed in the instrument itself by which it may be amended; but while it remains unaltered, it must be construed now as it was understood at the time of its adoption. It is not only the same in words, but the same in meaning, and delegates the same powers to the Government, and reserves and secures the same rights and privileges to the citizen; and as long as it continues to exist in its present form, it speaks not only in the same words, but with the same meaning and intent with which it spoke when it came from the hands of its framers, and was voted on and

---

[12] **tribunal**—court of justice, law court.

adopted by the people of the United States. Any other rule of construction would **abrogate**[13] the judicial character of this court, and make it the mere reflex of the popular opinion or passion of the day. This court was not created by the Constitution for such purposes. Higher and graver trusts have been confided to it, and it must not falter in the path of duty. . . .

And upon a full and careful consideration of the subject, the court is of opinion, that. . . . Dred Scott was not a citizen of Missouri within the meaning of the Constitution of the United States, and not entitled as such to sue in its courts; and, consequently, that the Circuit Court had no jurisdiction of the case, and that the judgment on the plea in abatement is erroneous. . . .

. . . [I]t appears affirmatively on the record that he is not a citizen, and consequently his suit against Sanford was not a suit between citizens of different States, and the court had no authority to pass any judgment between the parties. The suit ought, in this view of it, to have been dismissed by the Circuit Court, and its judgment in favor of Sanford is erroneous, and must be reversed.

But there is another point in the case which depends on State power and State law. And it is contended, on the part of the plaintiff, that he is made free by being taken to Rock Island, in the State of Illinois, independently of his residence in the territory of the United States; and being so made free, he was not again reduced to a state of slavery by being brought back to Missouri.

Our notice of this part of the case will be very brief; for the principle on which it depends was decided in this court, upon much consideration, in the case of *Strader et al.* v. *Graham* [1850]. In that case, the slave had been taken from Kentucky to Ohio, with the consent of the owner; and afterwards brought back to Kentucky.

---

[13] **abrogate**—abolish or repeal by authority; nullify.

And this court held that their status or condition, as free or slave, depended upon the laws of Kentucky, when they were brought back into that State, and not of Ohio; and that this court had no jurisdiction to revise the judgment of a State court upon its own laws. This was the point directly before the court, and the decision that this court had no jurisdiction turned upon it, as will be seen by the report of the case.

So in this case. As Scott was a slave when taken into the State of Illinois by his owner, and was there held as such, and brought back in that character, his status, as free or slave, depended on the laws of Missouri, and not of Illinois. . . .

Upon the whole, therefore, it is the judgment of this court, that it appears by the record before us that the plaintiff in error is not a citizen of Missouri, in the sense in which that word is used in the Constitution; and that the Circuit Court of the United States, for that reason, had no jurisdiction in the case, and could give no judgment in it. Its judgment for the defendant must, consequently, be reversed, and a mandate issued, directing the suit to be dismissed for want of jurisdiction.

QUESTIONS TO CONSIDER

1. What evidence do you find in Taney's words that he was a strong supporter of slavery who wanted to protect the South from northern attacks?

2. How did Taney argue that the decision against Dred Scott was, after all, in agreement with the Constitution?

3. Most Southerners defended their pro-slavery position by arguing for the Constitutional doctrine that put states' rights above national ones in all but a few, spelled-out situations. Yet, the Dred Scott decision overrode some states' rights. What are these?

4. In what way did the Dred Scott decision backfire against Taney's purpose?

Newspaper Editorials Respond

FROM THE ALBANY, NEW YORK, *EVENING JOURNAL* AND THE RICHMOND, VIRGINIA, *ENQUIRER*

The Supreme Court decision in the case of Dred Scott v. Sanford *prompted passionate outpourings from the editorial writers of papers in both the South and the North. Journalists expressed the views of most of their readers in the strongest language they could command. Thus, on March 10, 1857, the northern editorial writer for the Albany, New York* Evening Journal *called the decision "monstrous," while the southern journalist at the* Enquirer *in Richmond, Virginia, hailed it for rejecting the "diabolical doctrines" of anti-slavery "factionists and fanatics."*

Half a Million Citizens Disenfranchised

Albany, New York, *Evening Journal*
March 10, 1857

Many things in the monstrous decision of the U.S. Supreme Court shock the moral sense of the public.

But the barbarism of the blow which **annihilates**[1] the citizenship of all the Free colored people in the United States, has fallen with a stunning force on all who have been taught that justice is obligatory on man, and that Christianity is the social law of Humanity. The half million of men and women paralysed by the **atheistic**[2] logic of the decision of the case of Dred Scott, which **disenfranchises**[3] them on the soil on which they were born, will be to all free and uncorrupted souls a complete denial of the bad law and worse conscience, with which the Supreme Court has pronounced its departure from Republicanism and its entrance into Slavery.

The Dred Scott Case
Richmond, Virginia, *Enquirer*
10 March, 1857

In anticipation of the definitive decision of the Supreme Court of the United States in the Dred Scott case some months or more ago, its **adjudication**[4] was announced through a respectable proportion of the press, emanating, we do not now recollect precisely, whence or how; but, as the sequel shows, not from mere conjecture, or without reliable data, for it was then stated that seven of the nine judges constituting the court, agreed on the opinion that the Missouri Compromise was unconstitutional, and consequently, that the rights originating in it and under it, were even **factitious**[5] and ineffective. And it will be seen by the authentic annunciation of the grave and deliberate decision of that august body, in another column, that what was rumor then is reality now.—Thus

---

[1] **annihilates**—reduces to nothing; totally destroys.
[2] **atheistic**—denying the existence of God; ungodly.
[3] **disenfranchises**—takes the citizenship away from.
[4] **adjudication**—legal decision.
[5] **factitious**—causing dissension.

has a politico-legal question, involving others of deep import, been decided emphatically in favor of the advocates and supporters of the Constitution and the Union, the equality of the States and the rights of the South, in **contradistinction**[6] to and in repudiation of the diabolical doctrines **inculcated**[7] by factionists and fanatics; and that too by a tribunal of jurists, as learned, impartial and unprejudiced as perhaps the world has ever seen. A prize, for which the athletes of the nation have often wrestled in the halls of Congress, has been awarded at last, by the proper umpire, to those who have justly won it. The *nation* has achieved a triumph, *sectionalism* has been rebuked, and abolitionism has been staggered and stunned. Another supporting pillar has been added to our institutions; the assailants of the South and enemies of the Union have been driven from their *point d'appui;*[8] a patriotic principle has been pronounced; a great, national, conservative, union-saving sentiment has been proclaimed. An adjudication of the constitutionality of the Missouri Compromise, in the Dred Scott case, inseparably embraced **collateral**[9] questions of such character, as also to involve incidental issues, not unfrequently arising in the councils of the country, and which have ever proved, points of irreconcilable antagonism between the friends and enemies of the institutions of the South; all of which, it will be seen, have been unequivocally established in accordance with the sense of the Southern people. And thus it is, that reason and right, justice and truth, always triumph over passion and prejudice, ignorance and envy, when submitted to the deliberations of honest and able men: that the **dross**[10] and the genuine metal are separated when the ore is accurately assayed.

---

[6] **contradistinction**—distinction by contrast or opposition.

[7] **inculcated**—persistently taught; indoctrinated; implanted in the mind.

[8] *point d'appui*—French for a stronghold along a battle line.

[9] **collateral**—side by side; connecting.

[10] **dross**—waste or impure matter that rises to the surface of molten metals.

QUESTIONS TO CONSIDER

1. What, in your opinion, explains the difference between the views of these two newspaper editorial writers?

2. What principles do each of the editorial writers see upheld in the Dred Scott decision?

3. What language in these editorials might suggest the Civil War that was soon to break out over this issue?

Civil War and Freedom

African Americans in the Union Army The Civil War broke out in April, 1861, when Confederate forces attacked Fort Sumter, South Carolina. By May, Union General Benjamin Butler accepted runaway slaves at Fortress Monroe, Virginia, and put them to work, declaring them "contraband of war." A year later, General David Hunter, Union commander in the Sea Islands of South Carolina, requested permission to give black men arms and make them soldiers, but the War Department wasn't ready to take this step. By July, 1862, however, the Militia Act of Congress permitted men of African descent to serve and granted freedom to them and their families, if they belonged to owners not loyal to the Union. In August, recruitment began. By May of 1863, the Bureau of Colored Troops was formed in the War Department. By war's end, nearly ten percent of the Union forces were African American.

Background Band of the 107th U.S. Colored Infantry, November 1865.

▲

Contrabands Working for the Union Army The word *contraband* usually refers to the arms and other supplies captured in wartime. In the Civil War, it was used to refer to the escaped slaves who worked with the Union forces.

Former slaves were employed as teamsters (wagon drivers) in the Civil War.
▼

▲

Fugitive slaves entered Fortress Monroe, Virginia, seeking the protection of General Benjamin Butler, June 1861.

Thousands of slaves liberated themselves by packing up and crossing Union lines.

▼

The Emancipation Proclamation

BY PRESIDENT ABRAHAM LINCOLN

President Lincoln never said that ending slavery was the main objective of the Civil War. He insisted that his goal was to save the Union. Four border slave states—Maryland, Kentucky, Missouri, and Delaware—had stayed in the Union, and Lincoln did not want to lose them to the Confederacy. However, as the war went on, public opinion in the North shifted strongly in favor of emancipation. At a secret cabinet meeting on July 22, 1862, Lincoln presented a proclamation abolishing slavery. He was persuaded not to issue it until after a Union victory. When, on September 17, General George McClellan defeated the Confederates at the bloody Battle of Antietam, the time was right. On September 22, Lincoln issued the Emancipation Proclamation. It did not end slavery everywhere —the border states and the parts of the Confederacy controlled by the Union army were not included. But in all areas later occupied by the Union army, slaves were freed. And later, Missouri, in 1863, and Maryland, in 1864, voluntarily freed their slaves. Not until the Thirteenth Amendment was adopted in 1865, however, was slavery ended everywhere in the United States.

Whereas on the 22d day of September, A.D. 1862, a proclamation was issued by the President of the United States, containing among other things, the following, to wit:

"That on the 1st day of January, A.D. 1863, all persons held as slaves within any State or designated part of a State the people whereof shall then be in rebellion against the United States shall be then, thenceforward, and forever free; and the executive government of the United States, including the military and naval authority thereof, will recognize and maintain the freedom of such persons and will do no act or acts to repress such persons, or any of them, in any efforts they may make for their actual freedom.

"That the executive will on the 1st day of January aforesaid, by proclamation, designate the States and parts of States, if any, in which the people thereof, respectively, shall then be in rebellion against the United States; and the fact that any State or the people thereof shall on that day be in good faith represented in the Congress of the United States by members chosen thereto at elections wherein a majority of the qualified voters of such States shall have participated shall, in the absence of strong **countervailing**[1] testimony, be deemed conclusive evidence that such State and the people thereof are not then in rebellion against the United States."

Now, therefore, I, Abraham Lincoln, President of the United States, by virtue of the power in me vested as Commander-in-Chief of the Army and Navy of the United States in time of actual armed rebellion against the authority and government of the United States, and as a fit and necessary war measure for suppressing said rebellion, do, on this 1st day of January, A.D. 1863, and in accordance with my purpose so to do, publicly proclaimed for the full period of one hundred days from the first day above mentioned, order and designate as the States and parts of States wherein the people thereof, respectively, are this day in rebellion against the United States the following, to wit:

---

[1] **countervailing**—opposing.

Arkansas, Texas, Louisiana (except the parishes of St. Bernard, Plaquemines, Jefferson, St. John, St. Charles, St. James, Ascension, Assumption, Terrebonne, Lafourche, St. Mary, St. Martin, and Orleans, including the city of New Orleans), Mississippi, Alabama, Florida, Georgia, South Carolina, North Carolina, and Virginia (except the forty-eight counties designated as West Virginia, and also the counties of Berkeley, Accomac, Northhampton, Elizabeth City, York, Princess Anne, and Norfolk, including the cities of Norfolk and Portsmouth), and which excepted parts are for the present left precisely as if this proclamation were not issued.

And by virtue of the power and for the purpose aforesaid, I do order and declare that all persons held as slaves within said designated States and parts of States are, and henceforward shall be, free; and that the Executive Government of the United States, including the military and naval authorities thereof, will recognize and maintain the freedom of said persons.

And I hereby enjoin[2] upon the people so declared to be free to abstain from all violence, unless in necessary self-defense; and I recommend to them that, in all cases when allowed, they labor faithfully for reasonable wages.

And I further declare and make known that such persons of suitable condition will be received into the armed service of the United States to garrison forts, positions, stations, and other places, and to man vessels of all sorts in said service.

And upon this act, sincerely believed to be an act of justice, warranted by the Constitution upon military necessity, I invoke the considerate judgment of mankind and the gracious favor of Almighty God.

---

[2] enjoin—make an order (to refrain from doing some act). He is ordering the freed slaves not to resort to violence.

QUESTIONS TO CONSIDER

1. What were Lincoln's orders to the freed slaves?

2. What right did the Proclamation give the freed slaves?

3. What might be the reasons why certain places are exempted from the Proclamation?

4. What do Lincoln's comments in the final paragaraph suggest about his view of the Proclamation?

Freedom Letters

BY AARON OATS, LUCRETHIA OATS, AND JERRY SMITH

Thousands of black American men risked their lives during the Civil War, first by escaping their owners and then by enlisting in the Union army to fight in the service of their country. Many in the upper ranks of the military worked hard to help black soldiers locate and release their still-enslaved families both during and after the war itself. In Families and Freedom: A Documentary History of African-American Kinship in the Civil War Era, *historians Ira Berlin and Leslie S. Rowland collected material that shows how slaves struggled to preserve their families. The first of the three letters that follow was submitted by Aaron Oats, a former slave then serving in the Union army, to the office of the United States Secretary of War. The second is a note from Oats's wife Lucrethia, a Kentucky slave, and the third is a stinging letter of defiance to Aaron Oats from Lucrethia Oats's owner.*

U.S. Gen. Hospital, Hampten, VA **January 26, 1865**

Sir. I the under-Sined,[1] Respectfully ask for the liberation of my Wife and children now residing in the State of Ky. Boone County.

I enclose two letters Received from there one is supposed to be from my Wife the other is from a man claiming to be my Wifs master by the name of Jerry, Smith. You can see by the contents of his letter forbidding me not to write, Saying that he only gave her to me on my good conduct Of which he Says I have not fullfiled it is not necessary for me to say anymore you can see his letter,—

And as I am a *Soldier* willing to loose my life for my Country and the liberty of my fellow man I hope that you will please be So Kind as to attend to this please lett me know, or send me your Reply and oblige your humble Servent, yours very Respectfully

A L S

Aaron Oats

[First enclosure] [Union, Ky.] **December 22, 1864**

Dar husban I receive your letter dated December the 7 64 which gave me much pleasure to hear that you ar alive and well I mus state that I and mother and the children ar all well hopping thet these few lines may still find you well still I am at home and far as well as usial I shall content myself and wait for the time to come as you thought you could not get a **ferlough**[2] I must state that there is another one was Born sence you left but I suppose you heard of it if you have not I will tell you her name is effis tell [pood?] as they call him can run half as fast as you can and fat as ever your sisters ar all well Johns mother states that, she wish that John would right and if he wont Right when you right again send all the perticklers About him whether he is live or dead.

---

[1] The original spelling, capitalization, and punctuation of these three letters have been preserved. These writers used extra space to separate their sentences.

[2] **ferlough**—furlough, an official leave of absence.

N.B.[3] you stated in your letter that you sent me too letters and your picture but I never receivd either

so I must conclude my short letter by saing that I send my love to you all and keep the Best part for your self   so no more till death

HLSr

Lucrethia

[Second enclosure] [Union, Ky.]   *January 10, 1865*

When your letter came to hand it was red and answerd and when I went to put it in the office ther was another at hand Equal as insolent as the other so I concluded to send you a few lines apon my own responsibelity and, not to wright any more with out you will have some Respect for me   if you dont they will not be red nor answered my **darkes**[4] has too much Sence to be foold in such away   ther has been agreat menny woman and children have left and returned back again   one instant in my nabohood   Henry corben's mandy you nod her   dan had **encoyd**[5] her and six children over in cincinnati out on walnut hill and there she and three children starved to death   the oldest that could travel came home and got his master to bring them home to keep them from starvation and too of the youngest had ate flesh of ther fingers   NB Lucretia dont belong to you I only gave her to you for wife dureing good behaviour and you have violated your plede,   my darkes olways tells me when they want to leve me   they will tell me they say that if they ar to be deliberated they want it don honorable

---

[3] N.B.—note well. The initials stand for the Latin phrase *nota bene.*

[4] **darkes**—darkies, an insulting, racist term for slaves.

[5] **encoyed**—Smith may mean something like encouraged, or enticed and decoyed.

this lettere was rote the 22 of December but taken it back to answer you my self I neglected to put it in the office till now this being the 10 of January 1865 But my darkes is as well now as they wer then and doing better than when you was hear   now, they ar wated on when you was hear they had you to wait on so no more

HL

[Jerry Smith]

QUESTIONS TO CONSIDER

1. What outcome did Jerry Smith seem to expect for the Civil War? What reason might he have had for this expectation?

2. Upon what legal grounds did Smith claim that Lucrethia did not "belong" to Aaron Oats?

3. What do you think were Smith's real reasons for refusing Oats's request?

4. Based on the information you have here, what you know of the history of the Civil War, and your own life experiences, what do you think happened to Oats and his family? Explain your answer.

To My Old Master

BY JOURDON ANDERSON

The following letter is from a freed slave living in Ohio. It is addressed to his former master in Tennessee and written about 1865, the year the Civil War ended.

To My Old Master, Colonel P. H. Anderson
Big Spring, Tennessee

Sir: I got your letter, and was glad to find that you had not forgotten Jourdon, and that you wanted me to come back and live with you again, promising to do better for me than anybody else can. I have often felt uneasy about you. I thought the Yankees would have hung you long before this, for harboring Rebs[1] they found at your house. I suppose they never heard about your going to Colonel Martin's to kill the Union soldier that was left by his company in their stable. Although you shot at me

---

[1] Rebs—Rebel soldiers, Confederates. Jourdan is making a bitter joke. As his master had gone to kill a Union soldier hidden at Colonel Martin's, the Union soldiers should have hanged him for hiding Confederate soldiers.

twice before I left you, I did not want to hear of your being hurt, and am glad you are still living. It would do me good to go back to the dear old home again, and see Miss Mary and Miss Martha and Allen, Esther, Green, and Lee. Give my love to them all, and tell them I hope we will meet in the better world, if not in this. I would have gone back to see you all when I was working in the Nashville Hospital, but one of the neighbors told me that Henry intended to shoot me if he ever got a chance.

I want to know particularly what the good chance is you propose to give me. I am doing tolerably well here. I get twenty-five dollars a month, with **victuals**[2] and clothing; have a comfortable home for Mandy—the folks call her Mrs. Anderson—, and the children—Milly, Jane, and Grundy—go to school and are learning well. The teacher says Grundy has a head for a preacher. They go to Sunday school, and Mandy and me attend church regularly. We are kindly treated. Sometimes we overhear others saying, "Them colored people were slaves" down in Tennessee. The children feel hurt when they hear such remarks; but I tell them it was no disgrace in Tennessee to belong to Colonel Anderson. Many darkeys would have been proud, as I used to be, to call you master. Now if you will write and say what wages you will give me, I will be better able to decide whether it would be to my advantage to move back again.

As to my freedom, which you say I can have, there is nothing to be gained on that score, as I got my free papers in 1864 from the Provost-Marshal-General of the Department of Nashville. Mandy says she would be afraid to go back without some proof that you were disposed to treat us justly and kindly; and we have concluded to test your sincerity by asking you to send us our wages for the time we served you. This will make us forget and forgive old scores, and rely on your justice

---

[2] **victuals**—food.

and friendship in the future. I served you faithfully for thirty-two years, and Mandy twenty years. At twenty-five dollars a month for me, and two dollars a week for Mandy, our earnings would amount to eleven thousand six hundred and eighty dollars. Add to this the interest for the time our wages have been kept back, and deduct what you paid for our clothing, and three doctor's visits to me, and pulling a tooth for Mandy, and the balance will show what we are in justice entitled to. Please send the money by Adam's Express, in care of V. Winters, Esq., Dayton, Ohio. If you fail to pay us for faithful labors in the past, we can have little faith in your promises in the future. We trust the good Maker has opened your eyes to the wrongs which you and your fathers have done to me and my fathers, in making us toil for you for generations without **recompense**.[3] Here I draw my wages every Saturday night; but in Tennessee there was never any pay-day for the Negroes any more than for the horses and cows. Surely there will be a day of reckoning for those who defraud the laborer of his hire.

In answering this letter, please state if there would be any safety for my Milly and Jane, who are now grown up, and both good-looking girls. You know how it was with poor Matilda and Catherine. I would rather stay here and starve—and die, if it come to that—than have my girls brought to shame by the violence and wickedness of their young masters. You will also please state if there has been any schools opened for the colored children in your neighborhood. The great desire of my life now is to give my children an education, and have them form virtuous habits.

Say howdy to George Carter, and thank him for taking the pistol from you when you were shooting at me.

From Your Old Servant,

Jourdon Anderson

---

[3] **recompense**—payment for services performed.

QUESTIONS TO CONSIDER

1. What, in your opinion, could have been the reasons Colonel Anderson wrote asking Jourdon Anderson to return?

2. How can you tell whether or not Jourdon Anderson's offer to return to Colonel Anderson is a serious one?

3. What, if anything, does Jourdon Anderson miss about his life at Colonel Anderson's place?

4. What does Jourdon Anderson have now that he didn't have when he lived at Colonel Anderson's place?

5. How would you describe the letter to a friend?

Chronology

1619—A Dutch ship lands in Jamestown with its stolen cargo of kidnapped Africans. The Africans are sold for food.

1639—Maryland declares a Christian baptism does not make a slave free.

1641—Massachusetts becomes the first English colony to recognize slavery as a legal institution.

1662—". . . all children borne in this country shall be held bond or free only according to the condition of the mother. . . ."

1712— Rebellious slaves in the New York colony torch a building and kill nine white men.

1740—The Stono Rebellion is put down by a militia of armed planters.

1741–1742—New York justice Daniel Horsmanden heads an inquisition; the testimony of Mary Burton and others leads to the execution of over 100 slaves and free blacks.

1775—The American Revolution begins, and the British governor of the Virginia colony offers freedom to "all indentured servants, negroes, or others," who join His Majesty's Troops.

1778—George Washington and the Second Continental Congress offer freedom to slaves who fight in their army.

1781—The British lose the Battle of Yorktown, the final battle in the Revolution. A Federal Convention declares that Congress can choose to prohibit slavery in the territories.

1799—In the Petition of the People of Colour, seventy-one free blacks in Philadelphia petition Congress to acknowledge that all black people have the unalienable rights guaranteed in the Declaration of Independence and the Bill of Rights.

1800—Gabriel Prosser plots unsuccessfully to lead thousands of slaves against Richmond, Virginia.

1808—The Constitution's provision against the international slave trade takes effect. Slaves can no longer be brought in from Africa or other countries.

1818—Slave and non-slave states are equally balanced in the young nation.

1820—Congress passes the Missouri Compromise, admitting Missouri as a slave state, Maine as a free state (making twelve each), and forbidding slavery in the Louisiana Territory north of the latitude 36°30'.

1822—The Denmark Vesey Plot is uncovered in Charleston, South Carolina.

1831—Federal and state troops put down the Nat Turner Rebellion in Virginia.

1838—Angelina Grimké Weld and other abolitionists speak at the Second Annual Meeting of the Anti-Slavery Convention of American Women in Philadelphia while a jeering mob is gathered outside.

1840–1860—The Underground Railroad helps 1,000 slaves a year to escape.

1841—The Supreme Court rules that the Mendi mutineers of the *Amistad* are not escaped slaves but are kidnapped Africans. They are freed.

1845—Texas enters the nation as a slave state, upsetting the balance of slave and non-slave states.

1850—In the Compromise of 1850, California is admitted as a free state, the New Mexico and Utah Territories have no restrictions on slavery, and the Fugitive Slave Act fights back at the Underground Railroad with a vengeance.

1852—*Uncle Tom's Cabin*, by Harriet Beecher Stowe, is published.

1854—The Kansas-Nebraska Act undoes the Missouri Compromise by allowing the Territories to decide whether they will be slave or free. Slave holders rush into Kansas. Rival abolitionist and pro-slavery governments are set up. The riots that followed earn the state the name "Bleeding Kansas."

1857—In the *Dred Scott* decision, the Supreme Court rules that the Missouri Compromise is unconstitutional. Chief Justice Taney declares that all blacks, slaves or free, are not and cannot become citizens of the United States.

1859—Abolitionist John Brown attacks the Federal Arsenal at Harper's Ferry, Virginia.

1860—Abraham Lincoln wins the presidential election and South Carolina secedes.

1861–1865—Union forces fight Confederate forces in the Civil War.

1862—Lincoln issues the Emancipation Proclamation.

December 1865—Twenty-seven states ratify the Thirteenth Amendment and slavery is abolished in the United States.

ACKNOWLEDGEMENTS

Texts

12 "From *Roots*" by Alex Haley adapted from *Roots* by Alex Haley. Copyright © 1976 by Alex Haley. Used by permission of Doubleday, a division of Random House, Inc.

45 "The Middle Passage" by Daniel Mannix and Malcolm Cowley from "The Middle Passage", from *Black Cargoes* by Daniel P. Mannix with Malcolm Cowley. Copyright © 1962, renewed © 1990 by Daniel P. Mannix. Used by permission of Viking Penguin, a division of Penguin Putnam Inc.

50 "A Day on a Slaver" by Frederick M. Binder and David M. Reimers, from Frederick Binder and David M. Reimers, *The Way We Lived: Essays & Documents in American Social History, Third Edition*. Copyright © 1996 by Houghton Mifflin Company. Reprinted with permission.

64 "The First Africans" by Charles Johnson, Patricia Smith, and the WGBH series research team. Excerpts from *African In America, America's Journey Through Slavery* by Patricia Smith copyright © 1998 by WGBH Educational Foundation, reprinted by permission of Harcourt, Inc.

82 "Chattels Personal" by Kenneth M. Stampp. From *The Peculiar Institution* by Kenneth M. Stampp. Copyright © 1956 by Kenneth M. Stampp. Reprinted by permission of Alfred A. Knopf, Inc., a Divsion of Random House, Inc.

94 "Fighting for Britain in the American Revolution" by Charles Johnson, Patricia Smith, and the WGBH series research team. Excerpts from *African In America, America's Journey Through Slavery* by Patricia Smith, copyright © 1998 by WGBH Educational Foundation, reprinted by permission of Harcourt, Inc.

102 "Runaways and Punishment" by Edward Ball. Excerpt from "Bloodlines" from *Slaves In The Family* by Edward Ball. Copyright © 1998 by Edward Ball. Reprinted by permission of Farrar, Straus and Giroux, LLC.

107 "Slave Revolts." Excerpts from *African In America, America's Journey Through Slavery* by Patricia Smith copyright © 1998 by WGBH Educational Foundation, reprinted by permission of Harcourt, Inc.

130 "Day-to-Day Resistance" by Peter Kolchin. Excerpt from "Antebellum Slavery: Slave Life" from *American Slavery: 1619–1877* by Peter Kolchin. Copyright © 1993 by Peter Kolchin. Reprinted by permission of Hill & Wang, a divsion of Farrar, Straus and Giroux, LLC.

144 "African-American Language" by Nathan Irvin Huggins. From *Black Odyssey* by Nathan Irvin Huggins. Copyright © 1977 by Nathan Irvin Huggins. Reprinted by permission of Pantheon Books, a division of Random House, Inc.

152 "Plantation Days" by Mary Anderson. Excerpted from *My Folks Don't Want Me to Talk About Slavery*, edited by Belinda Hurmence, published by John F. Blair, Publisher. Reprinted with permission.

156 "Slave Marriages" by Herbert G. Gutman. From *The Black Family In Slavery And Freedom, 1750–1925* by Herbert Gutman. Copyright © 1976 by Herbert G. Gutman. Reprinted by permission of Pantheon Books, a division of Random House, Inc.

162 "The Slave Life Cycle" by Allan Kulikoff. From *Tobacco and Slaves: The Development of Southern Cultures in the Chesapeake, 1680–1800* by Allan Kulikoff. Copyright © 1986 by the University of North Carolina Press. Used by permission of the publisher.

201 "The Fugitive Slave Act in the North," from "Eric Foner on The Fugitive Slave Act in the North" from *Africans in America website*. Reprinted by permission of Eric Foner.

Images

Photo Research Diane Hamilton.

32–35 Courtesy of Jurgen Vollmer.

cover, 55–62, 121–129, 171–175, 220–223 Courtesy Library of Congress.

Every effort has been made to secure complete rights and permissions for each selection presented herein. Updated acknowledgements, if needed, will appear in subsequent printings.

Index